Fearless 365

Sandy Holly

Learn more about becoming a "Jesus Freak" at
www.JesusFreakApparel.com

Printed in the United States of America

DEDICATION

Fearless warrior, I dedicate this book to you. May you read, reflect, and become completely fearless.

If God is for us, who can ever be against us?
Romans 8:31

Contents

INTRODUCTION

It was the third week of December 2017 when I heard something on the television about the Bible's saying 365 times to "fear not." I had heard that before, so I dismissed it. A day later I was having coffee with a friend who also mentioned that fact to me. I brushed it off as "cool stuff" and a coincidence. Then I noticed my daily Bible readings all that week had "fear not" in the Scriptures. When Sunday rolled around, and the pastor mentioned that the Bible says "Fear not, have no fear, and do not be afraid" a total of 365 times, God finally had my attention! That day I had a big, old, ugly cry in church pew twelve. I also received my next assignment from God.

Ironically, as I first sat down to write *Fearless 365*, I was scared. "What do I know about being fearless?" I cried to God. "I don't know a thing about being fearless. I'm the girl who wrote the book, *More Jesus More Joy 365*. I know peace, love, and joy; I don't know fearless."

God quickly answered my plea for His leading and said, "Yes, you do. Every time you trusted Me with your life, your sadness, your spirit, you were fearless. Come with Me now; I am going to show you the rest. I will show you how to be completely fearless—leaving it all behind."

So I followed Him quickly, wide-eyed, and ready to learn every last detail from the fearless King. I quickly did as He asked. I read the Bible in six months, exploring, writing, and holding on to every last word. God showed me His awesome and majestic power, and then He showed me how to use it. Through this process, He showed me 365 ways to be fearless and how to live fearlessly.

First, I dug in and got serious, and let the Almighty God give me the lessons of a lifetime. Through my time spent with Him, I learned what fear is and how to become fearless in my everyday life. I learned to roar like a lion because I had the power of God available to me and running through me. I also learned how to deal with the evils that create the things I fear.

I learned to find my voice and roar. My roars were little at first—much like a baby cub testing her boundaries and her mother. Then I learned to really roar from the gut of my being. I belted out joyful, therapeutic roars against evil—even silent roars that pushed back evil and made the Devil shake and tremble.

Yep, me—the joy girl—learned to give a fearless roar and live a fearless life.

Living a fearless life is hard to do when we see fearful and disheartening reports every day in the news. I surely don't need to list them all here. We're all well aware of the evils we see daily. But seeing and hearing about the evils in this world *every* day creates a fearful nature in us, and that is right where Satan wants us—fearful in our day and filled with dread of the days to come. To understand the tragedies we're seeing weekly and sometimes daily on the news, we have to understand who Satan is. To understand fear, we first have to look at the character of Satan to see how evil operates.

Satan creeps into the weakest parts of our minds; nobody is exempt from his slithering access. For me, this starts with the way I talk to and think about myself. After I've allowed all the horrible things Satan calls me to become my truth, he has made his home. For me, his words become a familiar mix of melancholy and hatred. Then the evil moves from focusing on myself to the way I think about others. I sit in that mindset for a bit, and then it comes out of my mouth in hatred as gossip or slander of another, usually a close friend whom I love. Bam! Satan is in control!

When I realize I've given in to evil, I call it out fast, telling God all about it and confessing my wrongdoings to Him. Then Satan no longer has power and hold over me. I ask God for forgiveness and for Him to change my heart and my mind. He always does! But not everybody has a relationship with God, and that is where Satan's playground begins.

Let's look at those who are committing evil acts in this world, like the multiple mass shootings that make the news. Has the gunman allowed Satan into his hurts, pains, shortcomings, wrongs that have been committed against him, and the things he's done wrong to others? If so, he has given full reign over to Satan's evil power and has allowed Satan to confirm again and again all of the hatred that he's feeling. Life no longer is precious or special because Satan is in control.

No place is exempt for evil to enter after Satan is in control. You want to be upset and angry; good, you should be, but direct your anger at the real source—Satan. The Bible says in Romans 12:9 that we should hate evil but love one another. Don't point the finger at another to claim blame, just love. Put all the blame on Satan. When we truly and deeply love one another, Satan loses power. That is how we win this battle. We can conquer fear with love. We can clearly see Satan is coming after God's people. The truth is that we have free reign to choose good or evil. We have the ability to manifest our life's wounds or to release them to Jesus.

We have free reign to choose Jesus and be released and freed from Satan's hold on us.

Evil will always exist in this world, and that is scary, but I don't have to fear it. Whether I'm at a movie theater, a grocery store, a concert, school, or at work, if my life is taken, it was a life well-lived and well-loved because I've known Jesus. And I know who is waiting to accept me in Heaven. This world is not all there is; it will come to an end, but God is eternal and offers eternal life. When we understand that this earthly life is not all there is, we become excited for what will be and fearless for the time we live in it.

Knowing that, here's how He changed my view of fear. I know how the end of the story goes. A day is coming when Jesus will walk the earth in final victory. I know that no evil will exist in the new world. I know that the battle of good versus evil was already won long ago when Jesus chose the cross for us—all of us.

Since I know how the end of the story goes and have accepted the teachings of Jesus, I can remain fearless, knowing God has already gone before me and is fighting my battles. God is working out His plan.

God is just and will make things right. He will reward His faithful believers and punish the evil. When we're faced with trials and fear sets in, remember that God is in control; nothing surprises Him. I pray for the families who've lost loved ones due to the evils of the world. We, the believers and followers of Jesus Christ, know that their loved ones aren't really lost. They can be found in the waiting arms of Jesus in Heaven where there is finally no more pain and no more suffering.

In this life, God wants to use you and specifically designed you to make a difference in the world. He wants to strengthen you and give you the desires of your heart, but He can't do that if you remain in fear. When the hammer comes down, the gauntlet is thrown, and the rooster crows, He will not say, "I never knew you."

I can't wait for you to find your roar! Let's follow the fearless King and turn these pages daily to fear less and become Fearless!

Let's Roar!

Sandy Holly

Find Your Roar!

The wicked run away when no one is chasing them,
but the godly are as bold as lions. (Proverbs 28:1)

a lion, mighty among beasts,
who retreats before nothing. (Proverbs 30:30 NIV)

The lion has roared—
who will not fear?
The Sovereign LORD has spoken—
who can but prophesy? (Amos 3:8 NIV)

They will follow the LORD;
he will roar like a lion.
When he roars,
his children will come trembling from the west. (Hosea
11:10 NIV)

Then one of the elders said to me, "Do not weep! See, the
Lion of the tribe of Judah, the Root of David, has triumphed.
He is able to open the scroll and its seven seals." (Revelation
5:5 NIV)

The king's anger is like a lion's roar,
but his favor is like dew on the grass. (Proverbs 19:12)

They are like a lion hungry for prey,
like a fierce lion crouching in cover. (Psalm 17:12 NIV)

Stay alert! Watch out for your great enemy, the devil. He
prowls around like a roaring lion, looking for someone to
devour. (1 Peter 5:8)

Listen! Listen to the roar of His voice,

to the rumbling that comes from His mouth.
He unleashes His lightning beneath the whole heaven
   and sends it to the ends of the earth.
After that comes the sound of His roar;
   He thunders with His majestic voice.
When His voice resounds,
   He holds nothing back.
God's voice thunders in marvelous ways;
   He does great things beyond our understanding.

(Job 37:1-5 NIV)

Fear God above all; everything else get in line!

FOREWORD

"…You come against me with sword and spear…but I come against you in the name of the LORD…." (1 Samuel 17:45)

Here's the scene: David is walking around awkward in his new-to-him armor and shield. He needs only to take a few steps in them until he's deemed them of no value for him. He cannot use them for he's never tested this armor that is foreign to him. So he relinquishes the king's fine armor and goes with what he already knows will work for him. He has already honed and developed survival skills in the field and has become expert in their use.

David quickly drops the shield, removes the armor, grabs five smooth rounded stones, and puts them in his shepherd's bag. In reverting to what he knows, he is confident in the skills given to him by God. His dedication and practice has turned into protection from predators in the fields as well as a desire to protect and preserve the land of former generations.

David starts to walk toward Goliath with a God-given confidence and skill. Standing squarely before the giant Philistine, he removes a chosen stone from his bag, places it in his sling, and unerringly launches the projectile into Goliath's forehead, knocking him facedown to the ground.

David was so enamored by his great and mighty God that Goliath appeared little to him. God is greater than everything, and David knew it. He also knew God was with him, and He would not fail—like all the times God had been with him in the pasture as he tended and protected his sheep.

The story of David and Goliath is how God goes before us. This is how we hone and perfect the skills He has given us for battle. The shield and armor work for some but were not intended for all. Everyone is gifted differently by God; each is unique in His creation.

David obediently refined the skills God gave him. The battle was already won before David got on the scene, but he played a vital part in it because of his trust and faith in God. God goes before us; therefore, we have no fear!

GENESIS

Day 1: Read Genesis 9:1-17
The fear and dread of people being in charge will fall on all the living creatures.

Noah and his family have been given an invitation from God to advance to the top of the food chain. Here, God puts people in charge of everything—all the animals of the earth and the plants and vegetation. But along with this great responsibility come rules. We shouldn't be gluttonous or harmful to those beneath us; instead, we should be thankful and grateful for the food, remembering we will give an account for the life we lived and how we treated everything in our control. Are you mindful of the things you chose as food? Become fearless in seeking good food in a humane way.

Day 2: Read Genesis 15:1-6
God told Abram, "Do not be afraid."

When Abram received a vison from God, he was weary in heart and had many things on his mind about his future. The Lord said to Abram, "I am your shield and your great reward," encouraging His servant and reminding him that He will defend and bless him always. What worries or concerns do you have about your future? Trust that God has prepared your future for you. Take courage knowing He has gone before you as your shield and great reward. Become fearless about stepping into your future.

Day 3: Read Genesis 20:1-18
**Abraham thought there was no
fear of God in this place.**

Twice Abraham feared others more than God and lied to
protect his life. His wife Sarah was very beautiful, and he
feared that King Abimelech would have him killed to take
Sarah. He told the same lie earlier to the Egyptians. Even
biblical heroes fall short and allow fear to creep into their
lives. Have you ever lied for fear of the consequences?
Abraham was wrong; King Abimelech did fear God and
wasn't a wicked man. Deceiving others instead of trusting
God is not an easier way out. Become fearless in trusting God
can work in any unlikely situation.

Day 4: Read Genesis 21:1-21
**Do not be afraid; God has
heard the boy crying.**

Hagar was destitute and sobbing about her horrible situation.
She and her son were crying. God heard the boy and provided
for them. We do not need to be afraid to come to God with our
frightful situations. God is waiting to hear our cries and to
provide direction for us. Our situations won't seem as
formidable if we will let God handle them. What current
situation can you bring before Him today? Cry out to God and
ask for help. Become fearless in trusting that He will provide.

Day 5: Read Genesis 22:1-24
**Fearing God, Abraham did not
withhold anything from Him.**

God tested Abraham using his most beloved possession—his son Isaac. He passed God's test with flying colors, displaying complete obedience and trust in his heavenly Father, and he was rewarded. Abraham feared God enough to obey Him without question. He did not withhold his beloved son, and God spared Isaac's life and rewarded Abraham. When we obey and trust God, He uses and multiplies our resources. What part of your life and possessions are you withholding from God and His care? If He is asking you to use your resources, respond to Him in obedience and trust. Give it away! Then get ready to receive the blessings that He will give you. Become fearless in trusting God with your possessions.

Day 6: Read Genesis 26:17-32
Do not be afraid, for I am with you.

There is enough room for everyone in God's house. Quarrels with others will occur, but God's people choose peacemaking over conflict. God is with us, and we stay obedient and reverent to Him. We believers will be the ones to offer up an unexpected blessing to another instead of a fight. We learn to cooperate for the purpose of peace. How do you make peace in tough situations? Let go and compromise for peace. Become fearless in peacemaking.

Day 7: Read Genesis 28:10-22
Jacob was afraid when he realized the magnificence of God in this place.

Jacob realized God had allowed him see a vision in his dream. When he awoke, he was afraid and realized God was in this magnificent place. God told Jacob that his family line would be vast—like the sand or dust of the ground. Jacob started a relationship with God and made a covenant promise to follow, trust, and depend on Him. Jacob's descendants must also choose God on their own. As much as we'd like to, we cannot force someone to follow Jesus. They need to experience the magnificence of God in this place on their own. For whom do you regularly pray to choose Jesus? Just like Jacob decided, we believers have decided to follow Jesus, and we pray for others to join us. Become fearless in praying for others to choose Him.

Day 8: Read Genesis 31:1-55
Jacob fled in secret because he was afraid of Laban's wrath.

Jacob had worked hard for Laban for many years longer than he should have, all the while being deceived by him. The Lord told Jacob to return to the land of his relatives and He would be with him. When Jacob decided to leave, he became fearful and fled the scene instead of speaking up and trusting in God's provisions. Have you ever ran away instead of standing up for yourself? The only one we need to fear is God; no one and nothing can compare to God's force. Plant your feet firmly on the ground God gave you and take a stand. If God has asked you to do something, He has already made a way for you. Become fearless in follow the Lord's instructions.

Day 9: Read Genesis 35:1-29
Rachel's midwife reminded her not to be afraid as God was answering her prayer.

When Rachel gave birth to Joseph in Genesis 30:24, she asked God for another son. As this prayer was being answered, Rachel's midwife reminded her not to be afraid, for this was God's will. She encouraged her through her pain to be strong for God had given her another son. God hears our prayers and answers them in His perfect timing. He often answers our prayers in ways we can't understand above and beyond our imagination or asking. How has God answered your prayers beyond your understanding? God is in control, and His timing is to be respected. Become fearless in handing over your internal time clock to God.

Day 10: Read Genesis 42:1-5
Jacob was afraid to send his beloved gift from God.

When Jacob sent his children to buy grain in Egypt, he was afraid to send his youngest son. He was fearful because Benjamin was the only remaining tie to Rachel, his beloved wife who had passed. Jacob didn't want any harm to come to this special son. He was still hanging on to the past and not trusting God. What do you hold onto as tightly as Jacob? When we hold our possessions and gifts that God gave us so tightly, we don't allow space for God. Be grateful for the gifts God has given. Become fearless in trusting God with your possessions.

Day 11: Read Genesis 42:6-38
Joseph told his brothers that he feared God.

When Joseph saw his brothers, he immediately remembered his dreams about them. Joseph wanted to know if his youngest brother was alive, or if they had done away with him like they had tried to do to him. He told them to take the grain and bring back the youngest brother with them. Joseph reminded them that he was a man of God—a man of his word. If they did these things, they would live for Joseph feared God. Do you expect fair dealings from others, and are you fair with others? If you wholeheartedly fear God, you will not take advantage of any situation that profits you at the misfortune of another. Become fearless in being recognized as one who fears God.

Day 12: Read Genesis 43:15-31
Don't be afraid; your God has given you treasure.

Joseph's brothers were honest when they informed the steward of the returned coins in their sacks. Even though the men were frightened of the outcome, they chose to be honest. God is always working all things for our good because we believers love and honor Him with our actions. Have you ever told a white lie to keep the peace or make others feel better? Become bold in telling the truth because honesty and integrity is admirable to God. Become fearless in telling the truth.

Day 13: Read Genesis 46:1-7
I am with you; do not be afraid.

When God spoke to Israel (formerly Jacob), He reassured him to have no fear of his next move. God was with Israel. Feeling fear in new situations and making decisions is natural, but God wants us to know that He promises never to leave us nor forsake us. He is always with us; we will never fall. Maybe God isn't asking you to leave your home, but He is pursuing you for His designed kingdom purposes. What is God asking you to do that you have been fearfully reluctant to do? God is with you; do not be afraid! Become fearless in accomplishing your God-given task.

Day 14: Read Genesis 50:15-21
Don't be afraid; no one is in the place of God.

Joseph's brothers feared his retaliation now that their father had passed. When Joseph asked his brothers if they believed he was in the place of God, he was reminding them that his life was also guided by God. He reverenced God and was used by Him for such a time as this. Joseph chose forgiveness over revenge even though his brothers didn't deserve it. God forgives us every day even though we don't deserve it. What do you need in your life to become fearless and forgive? Throw your hands to the sky, and let God reign. Become fearless with forgiveness in your life.

EXODUS

Day 15: Read Exodus 1:1-22
The midwives feared God and disobeyed authority.

The midwives disobeyed the Pharaoh's orders to kill all of the male Hebrew babies. They feared God more than they feared man and let all the boys live. Because of their great faith, God rewarded the midwives with families of their own. Everyone will stand before God and give an answer for the life they lived, whether or not he or she is a believer. Have you ever been in a situation you had to go out of your way to choose God's law first and do the right thing? Take a faithful stand and live in such a way that honors and pleases God. Become fearless in following God's law first.

Day 16: Read Exodus 2:11-15
Moses was afraid of what became known by others.

Moses sinned and committed a crime. He thought no one had noticed until his deed became known by others. Even if no one sees our wrongdoings, God still does, and ultimately, we will have to answer to Him. Our sins and fears separate us from God. That we don't trust God with the things we fear in this life is an insult to Him. What wrongdoings have caused you to fear for yourself or others? Become fearless in doing what is always right.

Day 17: Read Exodus 3:1-14
Moses was afraid to look at God.

The crime that Moses had committed became known throughout his community; as a result, he was afraid and fled. Years later God wanted to use Moses, but he was so afraid he hid his face and couldn't even look at God. We, as believers, know that God is our friend. Though we approach God through friendship, He is holy, deserving of respect, and has all authority. How do you bring all of your sins—big and little—before the Lord and repent? God hears our cries and acts on our behalf. Become fearless in submission and gain freedom through His work.

Day 18: Read Exodus 14:1-29
Do not be afraid, stand firm, and you will see.

The Israelites were terrified as they saw the Egyptians coming. Even though they trusted God and had followed the directions of Moses, when trials came they doubted him and God's direction. God is bigger, and His plans are worked out for us so far in advance we can hardly understand. The Lord is our provider. What trials are you facing or have you faced that had you doubting God? Stand firm in the directions you are given from God. The Lord is fighting our battles. Become fearless when opposition strikes, and stand firm to the end.

Day 19: Read Exodus 15:1-21
All will hear how great God is, and the nations will tremble in fear.

The song that Moses and the Israelites sang to the Lord was one of pure joy and celebration from the victory they had experienced. God had protected them, providing an escape from their oppressors. Imagine being the Israelites as they watched the walls of water be restrained around them and crossing the Red Sea on dry ground. When word of this great feat spread, other nations trembled in fear of the greatness of God. Have you ever been so awestruck and joyful you broke out into song? God loves hearing from us in all forms of communication. Let the nations see the greatness of God through you. Become fearless in praising God publically.

Day 20: Read Exodus 19:1-25
The land and everyone in the camp trembled at the message from God.

A mysterious thick cloud reverberating with the sound of thunder and flashes of lightning covered the mountain where the Israelites were camped. Then the people heard a piercing trumpet blast that captured everyone's attention in the camp, causing them to tremble. God was making an entrance. He had something to say, and everyone knew it! Has God ever made an entrance like this into your life? Oftentimes, our salvation stories can be full of how God got our attention or pulled us out of the murky pit. Excitement to hear from God was mixed with fear because of His overwhelming power. Cling to His Words like the Israelites. Let Him captivate you always. Become fearless in devoting your attention to Him.

Day 21: Read Exodus 20:1-21
Do not be afraid; the fear of God will keep you from sinning.

God gave Moses the Ten Commandments as an instruction for righteous living. The Israelites trembled with fear at the majestic sights and sounds from the God of lightning and smoke. God was showing His power and authority and gave out the rules by which to live. We fear God when we don't obey these laws. If we repent of our sins against God, He forgives and loves us unconditionally. Can you look at God's law with love? God loves us enough to give us guidance and rules to live by. Become fearless in love for God's laws.

Day 22: Read Exodus 34:10-35
Moses' face was radiant, and the Israelites were afraid.

Each time Moses spoke with God, his face radiated from their time spent together. The Israelites were afraid and couldn't understand why his face was radiant, so Moses covered his face with a veil. We too need not be afraid to spend time with God. Have you seen others who light up a room from their time spent with the Lord? Go after that God-given glow by spending time with Jesus. You will radiate! Become fearless in your time with Jesus.

LEVITITCUS

Day 23: Read Leviticus 9:15-24
**People saw fire from the Lord
and fell facedown.**

When Aaron brought the sin offering of the people before the Lord, God appeared as fire and consumed it! What a mighty sight those people experienced! Theirs was joy mixed with fear. Back then, God showed physical acts of His power to His people. Today He shows His physical acts though His believers and counts on them to change the world through His power. Do you serve God as He intended or are you waiting on a mighty act? Take heart today knowing you are the mighty act and become fearless in serving the Lord.

Day 24: Read Leviticus 19:1-37
Fear your God, for He is the Lord of all.

The Lord gave Moses a mighty message to deliver to the people. In this message, God clearly said to fear Him for He is the Lord. God doled out all the "*do nots*" and listed various rules to guide the people's lives. God wasn't making up rules for fun; He was looking out for His people. Jesus later summed up these rules by simply telling people to love God and love others. When we do that, all of these rules fall into line and become easy to keep. Which of God's laws do you struggle with keeping? If we put love out front, it becomes first, and love with the help of God will guide our actions. View love as a rule. Become fearless in loving above all.

Day 25: Read Leviticus 25:1-38
Do not take advantage of each other, but fear God.

In the year of Jubilee, we are reminded by God that everything belongs to Him; we are merely caretakers of His property while we are here. When we start to view our life and our possessions in the way God created them, it becomes easier to share our life's work with others. Who is God asking you to help from the resources He has entrusted to you? Fear God, open your eyes to the needs of those around you. Become fearless in giving to others from the resources He has given you.

Day 26: Read Leviticus 26:1-13
I will grant peace, and no one will make you afraid.

The rewards we receive for being obedient to God are many. He gives us joy, peace, protection, food, and freedom from sin. Being set free from sin came at a cost that Jesus paid on our behalf. We, the believers, remember the sacrificial cost of our ultimate freedom and endeavor to live obedient lives to God giving thanks. Being aware that we could turn back to our sinful nature, how do we continually receive God's blessings? No turning back! Become fearless in receiving God's rewards for obedience.

Day 27: Read Leviticus 26:14-46
I will bring upon you sudden terror.

God displayed the punishment given to the Israelites for disobedience—unless they confessed their sins. God gave them the opportunity to repent of their sins, just as He gives us today. We can remain in terror of God for our unconfessed sins, or we can repent and ask for forgiveness. When we repent of our sins, we learn a lesson—sometimes a hard one. Either way, we experience growth as a result. After all, continual growth and a deeper relationship with Him is what God wants from His believers. What lessons have you learned from repenting of your sins? Ask God daily for forgiveness of wrong thoughts or actions. Become fearless in repentance.

NUMBERS

Day 28: Read Numbers 11:1-20
**The Lord's anger was aroused, and He
sent fire among them.**

The Israelites were complaining to each other about only eating manna. They craved the variety of foods they once enjoyed in Egypt. Since they were only complaining to each other and not taking their concerns to God, His anger was aroused! He sent fire down on their camp. Moses then took their complaints to God, and His anger subsided. God responded to Moses and answered his request. We must remember to seek God first and stop complaining to each other. When another complains to you, don't join in; take the person's complaints to the Lord. Become fearless in going to the Lord first.

Day 29: Read Numbers 12:1-16
Why then were you not afraid to
speak against Moses?

Jealousy gives us false strength, and oftentimes we act fearless and foolish because of that bogus confidence. Miriam and Aaron were jealous of Moses and wondered why the Lord only spoke through him. Instead of attacking the qualities of their brother, they attacked the character of his wife. Rather than face their problem of jealousy, they chose to make problems for Moses. Have you ever argued with someone over a non-issue because of your jealousy of something else? When we are unjustly criticized, consider it may have nothing to do with you at all; therefore, react in humility. God used Moses because he was the meekest man on earth. Become fearless in humility.

Day 30: Read Numbers 14:1-12
The Lord is with us; do not be afraid of them.

The Israelites' prayers were finally answered; the Promised Land was theirs to appropriate. However, upon seeing the land, they didn't trust God; they only feared the people. In the last leap of faith to enter the land God was handing over to them, they grumbled in fear and refused to go. When were you afraid to do something that God had clearly made a way for? God has provided for you in every area of your life, and He is with you in your fears. God is bigger than our greatest fears. Become fearless in always trusting God.

Day 31: Read Numbers 21:21-35
Do not be afraid; I handed him over to you.

The Lord handed over the defeat of the Amorites to Moses before the battle was even begun. Our God is stronger than anything. He fights our battles even before we know we're going to war. Oftentimes our battles aren't against people; they're against our own sins. Have you ever been at war with yourself? Remember that God is fighting for you and believe He will deliver you a victory! Become fearless in victory.

DEUTERONOMY

Day 32: Read Deuteronomy 1:9-18
Do not be afraid of any person for God is the ultimate Judge.

The same rules and guidelines God gave Moses to live by are the same rules that apply to us today. Along the way God saw that the leadership responsibilities became too much for Moses to bear alone, so He appointed others to help lift the burden and to assist Moses. When have you needed help in the workplace, the home, or in friendships? Don't be afraid to choose wise counsel and ask for help. We were created to be in community together, to help and love one another as ourselves. Become fearless in working together.

Day 33: Read Deuteronomy 1:19-25
Do not be afraid or discouraged.

When the spies returned, they deemed the land as being unworthy of the effort to claim it. God was handing the Promised Land to the Israelites, but they were too afraid of the risk and obstacles. In their rebellion, they were so filled with fear and their own will, they couldn't see the will and the power of God. When have you let a difficult situation bring fear into your life? Do not be discouraged; rather, become encouraged as God always goes before His faithful followers. Become fearless in courageous faith.

Day 34: Read Deuteronomy 1:26-46
Do not be afraid of them; the Lord is going before you.

The Israelites had to make a decision to trust God and move into the Promised Land or to rebel as a result of focusing on the obstacles to overcome and the negative situation. We become paralyzed in fear when we only focus on the negative consequences. Have you ever become immobilized with fear? When we follow God's lead, we trust that He has gone before us and is providing a way for us. Become fearless in focusing on the positive outcome.

Day 35: Read Deuteronomy 2:1-23
Your enemies will be afraid of you, but be careful not to provoke them.

While the Israelites were wandering in the desert, God gave them permission to pass through enemy territory, the hill country of Seir. God instructed them to be careful, respectful, and not to start a fight. God was with them, so they had no fear. The enemy nations were terrified for they knew God was with the Israelites. Neither do we have to worry about our enemies because God is on our side. How do you face each day living justly among others—even those who oppose you? Treat your enemies as God instructed the Israelites. Become fearless in the blessed assurance of God.

Day 36: Read Deuteronomy 2:24-37
God put terror and fear of you on all the nations.

When the Israelites walked the land, the Lord encouraged them. He told them other nations feared them even though they were ordinary people among giants. On their own they could've been easily overtaken, but with God they were untouchable by their enemies. Those who oppose God fear His faithful followers. Just as God told Moses the nations will fear the Israelites, He has told the world about us! Who is your enemy? Call him out by name today and ask the Lord to intervene. Do not fear your enemies for God is on your side. Become fearless in opposition.

Day 37: Read Deuteronomy 3:1-20
The Lord told them not to be afraid;
He has intervened.

The Lord delivered a message to the Israelites and told them not to be afraid of King Og and his mighty army. Even though the Israelites were vastly outnumbered, the Lord had already decided the fate of this war and had determined the Israelites would win. Imagine the self-confidence the Israelites displayed fighting with the confidence of God. This is the very same confidence God speaks into those believers who seek Him. Do you seek God first for help with your biggest problems—the kind you think are hopeless? Ask God to show up to give direction and the confidence to overcome. We face no problems that are too big for God to intervene and conquer. Become fearless in asking God to intervene in the impossible.

Day 38: Read Deuteronomy 3:21-29
Do not be afraid; the Lord is fighting my battles.

The Lord allowed Moses to see but not enter the Promised Land. Leaders will administrate and direct for a time and then pass on the baton to the next appointee. Moses strengthened and encouraged Joshua to lead the Israelites into the land God was handing over to them. God went before them and fought the evil they encountered. Have you witnessed the fighting power of the Lord? Whether you are being tempted or fighting the battle of your life, do not be afraid; the Lord is fighting your battles. Become fearless in the confidence of the Lord.

Day 39: Read Deuteronomy 5:28-33
**Their hearts would want to fear God
and keep His commandments.**

God told Moses that He *wanted* His people to fear Him—not because they had to, but because they *wanted* to obey and respect Him. The people would keep His commands out of deep love and admiration for God. Have you dedicated yourself wholeheartedly to the Lord? Total dedication is *wanting* to obey God out of deep love and respect—not because you have to fear God but because you *want* to. Become fearless in *wanting* to fear God in obedience.

Day 40: Read Deuteronomy 6:1-9
**Teach your children, and their children
may fear the Lord.**

Before the Israelites passed into the Promised Land, Moses wanted them to know the importance of teaching about God to this generation and the next. Moses encouraged the people to hold fast in their belief of the one true God. He also reminded them that throughout their daily activities to continually teach their families the commandments taught to them in the desert. Do you talk with your family daily about God and what He's done throughout your day? Reminding each other who God is, what He's done in your life, and where He's leading you next is so important. This generation and the next will be watching. Become fearless in teaching the next generation.

Day 41: Read Deuteronomy 6:13-25
Fear the Lord and take an oath in His name.

Moses warned the people to take an oath in the name of the Lord and fear only Him. An *oath* is "a promise, a pledge, or a vow to do something." Moses encouraged the people to take an oath of the commandments that had been taught to them in the desert. Today, make your own oath and statement regarding God's commandments and promise to honor those laws. Can you write out the Ten Commandments without looking them up? Impress them on your heart and mind. Become fearless in your promise to the Lord.

Day 42: Read Deuteronomy 7:1-26
Do not be afraid of them; remember I am your God.

God told the Israelites that He would completely destroy their evil enemies even though they were bigger and stronger and hand over the people and their possessions. The Lord chose to drive out the enemy nations little by little instead of all at once. God often works in our lives the same way. Perhaps we cannot handle all of the lessons at once. God has the power to deliver all of the lessons and victories at once, but we might not be able to keep up. What lessons and topics has God handed to you a little at a time? Little by little, look for the victories that God is handing over to you. Become fearless in expecting a victory from God.

Day 43: Read Deuteronomy 9:7-29
Moses feared the anger and wrath of God would destroy the people.

God had just given Moses the Ten Commandments, and the leader of the Israelites knew the importance of worshipping only God. After God told Moses his people had cast a gold idol to worship in his absence, he ran down the mountain in fear and crushed the Ten Commandments to pieces. In the absence of leadership, the people began making up their own rules and sinned greatly against God. We need the leadership of those who have dedicated their life to learning Scripture and communicating with God. Who in your daily life mentors your spiritual walk with Jesus? Having a leader and a mentor in your life for guidance is so important. Become fearless in seeking a devout mentor.

Day 44: Read Deuteronomy 10:12-22
God asks you to fear the Lord and walk in His ways.

Moses clearly recaps that what God asks of us and pleasing Him is not complicated. To fear God is to respect, follow, love, serve Him with your whole being, and obey His commandments. Have you ever confused these by adding other non-essential rules to His list? Don't let other's rules or requirements about God become your own. Become fearless in completing *only* what God has asked.

Day 45: Read Deuteronomy 11:1-32
**No one can stand against you; the Lord has put
the fear of you on the whole land.**

To love and obey the Lord has great rewards. The Lord
promised the people if they obeyed the commands He had
given and always teach them to their children, He would instill
fear in their enemies and drive out all the other nations
everywhere they went. God still does this for His believers. He
goes before us into the boardroom, on the ball field, and into
battle. Just like the Israelites, we too have a choice today—to
obey the Lord or accept the fate of our disobedience. How has
the Lord rewarded your obedience this week? The Lord will
go with us everywhere He's invited. Become fearless in
recognizing His rewards.

Day 46: Read Deuteronomy 20:1-9
Do not be terrified and give in to panic.

Fear breeds fear, which is why the officers asked if any
members were afraid to go into battle. If so, they were allowed
to leave so that the contagion of fear did not spread through
the ranks. Has fear of a certain situation kept you from
missing out on what turned into an awesome blessing? Fear
can rule us and take over if we don't put our trust in God.
Remember God is our security, and He has already gone
before us. Don't give fear a foothold. Become fearless today
in any situation presented to you.

Day 47: Read Deuteronomy 28:1-14
You are called by the name of the Lord;
the people will fear you.

Moses was warning the people that they have now become the people of the Lord. They are to obey and keep the laws given to them, and they will be greatly blessed by God. The other nations of people will see the Lord is with the Israelites, and they will fear them. The Israelites prospered when they were obedient to the Lord. When have you been rewarded by God for your obedience to Him? Serving God doesn't go unnoticed. Others can see our faith in God by our actions and the way we live. Become fearless in living for the Lord and impacting others.

Day 48: Read Deuteronomy 29:1-29
The Lord's wrath burned against those
who abandoned the covenant.

Moses encouraged the people to renew God's covenant in their lives. He urged the people not only to know God's Word, but to obey it in their lives. Knowing and obeying Scripture makes a difference in our daily lives. Others can see who Jesus is and what living biblically looks like. One at a time we can build God's kingdom in our work place, neighborhoods, and especially in our families. Does your community, co-workers, friends, and family know you obey the Word of God? Declare your faith for all to see. You may be the only walking Bible some people will ever see. Become fearless in living out Scripture.

Day 49: Read Deuteronomy 31:1-8
Be strong and courageous; do not be afraid.

Moses wasn't permitted to enter the Promised Land. The Lord also told Him he would no longer lead the people. Even though Moses was probably disappointed, he was still full of obedience and love for God. He chose to strengthen the next leader and speak truth to him. Moses prepared Joshua with the pep talk of a lifetime. Has anyone spoken truth to you about your life? Paying attention to God's promptings for our own life and also for others is so important. The Lord has told us and He has gone before us; therefore, we must trust, obey, and encourage others in His lead. Become fearless in strengthening others.

Day 50: Read Deuteronomy 32:1-47
Their fathers did not fear God.

In this song, Moses describes God's love for His people and condemns their lack of trust and fear of Him. Even if our families and the generations in our family line choose not to fear God, we still can today. Our salvation in Jesus Christ is based on our relationship with Him, not others. We share the gospel with others so nobody gets left behind. Who in your family do you pray doesn't get left behind? Fervently pray for those who do not fear God. Call them by name and ask God to intervene; trust that He will. Become fearless in praying down the names of those who do not fear God.

JOSHUA

Day 51: Read Joshua 1:1-9
Do not be discouraged; the Lord will be with you wherever you go.

Joshua took over leading the children of God after the death of Moses. In his new job, he assumed an abundance of responsibilities and new challenges. Trying to tackle life's circumstances without God's help or leading can be daunting and terrifying. With God, becoming a leader can be a great adventure as Joshua would discover. What in your life has been your biggest challenge? God is with us wherever we go and in all of life's situations. Allow God to be with you and lead you. Become fearless in life's challenges.

Day 52: Read Joshua 2:1-24
The people are melting in fear because of you.

Joshua sent two spies into the Promised Land to scope out the land and return with a plan of attack. The spies met Rahab, a prostitute living in Jericho, who was helpful to them and saved their lives. Rahab, who had a minimal knowledge of God, knew His excellence, feared Him, and risked all for Him. Have you ever assumed something about someone with whom you've never spent time? Don't assume someone's interest or lack of interest in God by the person's appearance or lifestyle. Become fearless in accepting others.

Day 53: Read Joshua 4:1-24
He did this so you would see His power
and fear the Lord always.

The Lord spoke to Joshua who then commanded each of the twelve tribes of Israel to go back into the middle of the Jordan where the ground was still dry and gather a stone. They built a monument stacking the stones where they had camped the first night. The stones were a symbol for all to see and remember the great power of God, who stopped the flow of water for His people. How have you seen the power of God with your own eyes? When we remember His great power, we also remember that we are weak in our own power without God. Become fearless in harnessing the great power of God.

Day 54: Read Joshua 7:1-13
After this defeat the people's hearts melted
and became like water.

Joshua sent his troops into battle without seeking God first. In doing so, he was relying on his own wisdom and the strength and power of the nation of Israel. God was not with them because of their sin. Achan broke the covenant by stealing hallowed things and then lying about the theft. Only after suffering the defeat did Joshua fearfully cry out to God in prayer for His help. What sins in your life are keeping you from God? Do you seek Him first or only when your life is in turmoil? Our sin separates us from God. Take the steps to align your life to His covenant. Become fearless in seeking God first.

Day 55: Read Joshua 8:1-29
The Lord spoke to Joshua and told him
not to be afraid or discouraged.

After Joshua's repentance and Israel's confession of sin, God forgave the people, strengthened them, and prepared them for battle. The Lord was with Israel and gave the orders to Joshua to take the land of Ai. They conquered Ai the second time with the Lord's help. When we include God's direction in our life and do things with His help and strength, He gives us great victories. What have you failed at doing on your own, and what victories have you experienced with the Lord's help? We lose when we give up and fail to include God. Become fearless in never giving up.

Day 56: Read Joshua 9:1-27
We feared for our lives because
of you and did this.

Out of fear, the Gibeonites deceived Joshua and tricked him into making an oath before God. Joshua made the treaty of peace with them without inquiring of God. We must be slow in our actions, inquiring of God and waiting on Him to answer. Because we follow God, opposition will strike us in a myriad of ways. Staying in constant communication with God helps us to be wise in our actions. When have you made a seemingly insignificant decision about some matter that later turned out to be a big deal? Include God in the big and little details of life. Become fearless in constant communication with God.

Day 57: Read Joshua 10:1-15
Do not be afraid; I have given them into your hand.

When the Gibeonites were overtaken and in need of help, Joshua showed his mighty integrity and trust in others. He trusted God to deliver another great victory just as He said. Even though the Gibeonites deceived him once, Joshua was true to his word and came to their rescue. How often have you really forgiven someone, let it go, and moved on in relationship with them? If you have forgiven someone, keep your word and let it go. Trust God, and don't keep track! Become fearless in forgiveness.

Day 58: Read Joshua 10:16-28
Joshua reminded them not to be afraid or discouraged.

Joshua reminded the Israelites of the Lord's words not to be afraid or discouraged, but to be strong and courageous. He reminded them of the protection from God in the past and the great victories they were given though Him. Do you often forget the power of God in your life? We need to remember how God has helped us in the past and remember He will help us in our current or next situation. Become fearless in remembering God.

Day 59: Read Joshua 11:1-15
Do not be afraid of them; let Me show you
what I am about to do.

The Lord again reminded Joshua not to be afraid of the enemy. Then the Lord again brought about a victory for Israel because of their obedience to God. An individual has the choice to obey God. Complete obedience to God is obeying Him in every area of your life. Have you ever been obedient to God with one thing but not another? Maybe you give Him your time but not your resources. Mindfully obey all of the instructions given by God. Become fearless in total obedience to God.

Day 60: Read Joshua 14:1-15
My brothers made the hearts of
the people melt with fear.

Caleb was faithful to God early in his journey and throughout his life. God noticed and rewarded him for his faithfulness by giving him an inheritance in the Promised Land. Caleb wholeheartedly trusted, honored, and worshiped God. Nothing was absent from his faithfulness. Do you become fearful when others are? The believers of Jesus Christ don't live in fear; they live in wholehearted faith. Become fearless today in your faithfulness to God.

Day 61: Read Joshua 22:1-34
Your descendants might cause ours
to stop fearing the Lord.

When the tribes of Reuben, Gad, and the half-tribe of Manasseh built an altar to the Lord, the rest of Israel feared they were rebelling against God. The altar was a memorial for future generations to see and remember they all worshiped the same God. It was built as a reminder for the next generation to see all that God has done in their lives. What traditions do you maintain that reminds your family and the next generation about God? Prepare the way for future believers. Become fearless in establishing traditions for the next generation.

Day 62: Read Joshua 23:1-16
Be strong and carefully obey all of the laws.

Joshua's final message to the leaders was to be very strong in their weaknesses. He knew his people's weaknesses just like God knows ours. Joshua encouraged them and reminded them of the way to go and to obey all the laws. In which area of weakness would God remind you to be very strong? Identify your weaknesses and ask for God's help to overcome them. Become fearless in knowing and improving your weakness.

Day 63: Read Joshua 24:1-27
Fear the Lord, and serve Him faithfully.

Joshua was encouraging the people to throw away their past foolishness of worshipping other gods. They had to decide to throw away all inhibitions and to wholeheartedly serve the Lord or serve false gods. Have you chosen the Lord, or are you quietly rebelling in an area of your life? God proved Himself daily to the Israelites just as He does for every believer today. Declare Him as your very own every day of your life. Become fearless in choosing God over and over again.

JUDGES

Day 64: Read Judges 6:1-40
Peace to you, do not be afraid, for you are safe.

God knows our hearts and exactly what we're going to say before we even say it. God knew Gideon's fears when he thought he would die from seeing an angel of the Lord face to face. God gave him immediate peace by telling him not to be afraid; he wasn't going to die. Gideon was referring to Moses' words in Exodus 33:20 about no one seeing the face of God and living. He thought seeing an angel of the Lord would have the same result, but God gave him peace. When was the last time God immediately gave you peace in your fears? God gives us strength, peace, and freedom when we fearlessly follow Him. Become fearless in following God who knows us completely.

Day 65: Read Judges 7:1-8
Those who tremble in fear may turn back.

The Lord was making a point to remind us that we cannot complete His tasks in our own strength. By sending back the fearful soldiers and reducing number a second time, he made sure the victory would only be given by God's help and hand. Gideon's soldiers were outnumbered and couldn't possibly win the battle in their own strength. The soldiers could not take credit for their victory; God would have to intervene. In what battle did you clearly win through God's strength? We need God's guidance in our daily lives so that no one can boast and say, "Look what I have done!" Become fearless in seeking daily victories through His strength.

Day 66: Read Judges 9:1-57
**Jotham fled because he was afraid of
the power of his brother Abimelech.**

Abimelech craved power and became a king who misused his power and influence. Because God alone appoints and assigns all positions of power, the choice is to handle the power and position in a way that is pleasing to Him. Three years had passed while God waited for Abimelech to use his power in the proper way. When he didn't comply, God removed him from his position. God deals with sin and misuse of power in His own time. He gives us all time to change, repent, and get back on track. What gracious amount of time has God given you to repent and change something? Thank God we don't get what we deserve immediately; He allows us time to choose to make it right. We don't know what tomorrow brings, so make things right with God today. Become fearless in recognizing the gift of time.

RUTH

Day 67: Read Ruth 3:1-18
Don't be afraid; I will do all that you ask.

Ruth fully trusted her mother-in-law, Naomi, following her instructions without knowing the outcome. She was probably scared to enter the threshing floor after all of the women had left for the evening, but she obeyed because she trusted Naomi's wisdom. Have you ever had a friend or family member you trusted and loved enough to follow their guidance into the unknown? Be willing to listen to the advice of the wise. God brings wise people into our lives to speak truth to us. Become fearless in trusting wise people.

1 SAMUEL

Day 68: Read 1 Samuel 3:1-21
Samuel was afraid to tell Eli the bad news.

Nothing gets past God; even if we overlook things, He doesn't. Failing to rightfully address or ignore our own sin or the sins of others affects the kingdom. Neglect allows the evil of sin to exist in our lives. When God spoke to Samuel, He revealed what would happen to the high priest and his family line because of Eli's failure to confront the sins of his family, thereby sinning himself. Samuel was afraid to tell Eli, his mentor, the bad news. Have you ever become so busy with work or even kingdom work that you neglected your own family and friends? Speak truth today and follow up the truth with Godly actions. Become like Samuel who had the right priorities, and be ready to speak truth—even when it's hard to do. Become fearless in speaking truth.

Day 69: Read 1 Samuel 4:1-11
The Israelites' enemies were afraid because the Lord had come into the camp.

When the Philistines heard the great shouts and saw the ark of the covenant returning to the Israelite camp, they were afraid. Their fear came from the terrible plagues God brought to the Egyptian people when they were against the Israelites. The Israelites mistakenly believed the ark was the source of their power—not God. Therefore, they used the ark as a type of insurance policy against their enemies. The Israelites were far from God even though the ark was in their camp. God was far from their hearts. Have you ever gone through the motions of Christianity, showed up at church, or only prayed when you needed help? God is not our insurance policy when things go wrong in our lives. He's our endurance policy for everyday life! He adores you! Become fearless in keeping God close.

Day 70: Read 1 Samuel 7:1-17
When the Israelites heard of the attack, they were afraid.

The Israelites were afraid of being attacked by the Philistines and asked Samuel to cry out to God on their behalf. He did, and after the great victory, he set up an Ebenezer, a large stone memorial, as a reminder of the great day the Lord had provided victory. Did you ever set up a memorial honoring God for what He has done in your life? Having our own memorial of a past victory helps us to remember what God has done for us. In times of fear, we can turn to our past victories and gain strength, knowing God will provide for us again. Become fearless in remembering what God has done.

Day 71: Read 1 Samuel 11:1-15
The Lord's terror fell on the people.

Saul burned with anger of the mistreatment of his fellow Israelites and reacted in such a way that terror and fear fell on the people. Anger can cause both healthy and unhealthy reactions in and from people. Anger expressed at sin or at the mistreatment of others is normal behavior. The Bible states numerous times that hatred of sin is not wrong. How we carry out our anger matters to God. How have you reacted emotionally in anger only to regret it later? We need to take our anger to God and ask Him to show us how to direct it to bring about positive change. Do not surrender to defeat. God always rescues His people. Become fearless in taking your anger to God.

Day 72: Read 1 Samuel 12:1-25
Be sure to fear the Lord and serve Him faithfully with all your heart, all your days.

In Samuel's farewell speech, he emphatically reminds the people that they must always fear the Lord, and it will be well with them. If they don't, God's hand will be against them. The magnificent and unusual rainfall showed the people God was displeased with them. They realized the sin they had committed by asking for a king to reign over them, instead of accepting God as their true King, and they were afraid. Was there ever a time you thought something was better than what God was already offering you? Take time to consider all the great things God has given and done for you. Become fearless in holding fast to God, the one true King.

Day 73: Read 1 Samuel 13:1-22
Saul's troops were quaking with fear.

The Israelites were quaking with fear at the sight of their opposition. They forgot God was always with them. Saul quickly learned a hard lesson from acting impatient and not seeking the Lord first. When life's toughest battles happen, forgetting that God is our help is easy. Instead of turning to Him, we try to handle life's battles on our own. When have you entered opposition on your own, forgetting God? In our own strength, we will rarely win; in His strength and help, we will always win. Become fearless in trusting God's help.

Day 74: Read 1 Samuel 15:1-35
Saul was afraid of the people and gave in to them.

God gave Saul, the newly anointed king, strict orders, but he failed to complete the task. In fear, Saul gave into his men and rebelled against God. When we give in to others in modern-day times, our giving in may appear as simple as not praying before a meal in order to please non-believers. However, we must obey God and honor Him at all times. Obeying God is more important than pleasing man. When have you disobeyed God to please others? At times it seems easier to please friends and family, but we will suffer long-term for not obeying God's commands. We will be with God for all of eternity; we may not be with man forever. Become fearless in obeying God in all situations.

Day 75: Read 1 Samuel 16:1-13
The elders trembled when they met Samuel.

Samuel, a prophet of the Lord, obeyed and went to Bethlehem to find the next one God would anoint as king. The elders of the town went out to meet him, fearing that he did not come in peace. Samuel did not denounce them for their sins; rather, he assured the people he was there to anoint God's next king. God instructed Samuel to anoint David, the youngest and the least qualified to be king. God doesn't look at the same outward appearance that man does; He looks at the heart. Many were surprised when David was anointed king. Have you ever been surprised by someone God placed into service or into your life? How did it turn out? Nothing happens without God's consent. Trust Him! Become fearless in welcoming God's surprises.

Day 76: Read 1 Samuel 18:1-30
When Saul saw David's success,
he was afraid of him.

David successfully completed every task Saul gave him because God was with the future king. The people saw David's success and loved him; they praised him with song and danced to celebrate his victories. Saul became very jealous of David's success and planned his demise. David continued to be humble and lead his people. Have you ever had jealous people attack you in some way? How did you handle the situation? Even during Saul's hateful attacks, David chose to love his king and show him kindness. Befriend those who oppose you, and when the Lord gives you success, stay humble and give the glory to God. Release your foolish pride! Become fearless in remaining humble.

Day 77: Read 1 Samuel 21:1-15
David was very much afraid and pretended to be insane before King Achish.

David fled to Gath to escape Saul's hot pursuit. There, the servant of King Achish asked David if he were the mighty warrior about whom all the songs were sung. David became very frightened that he was known and pretended to be insane to protect himself because no one would harm a mentally impaired person. His ruse worked, and he escaped from Gath and hid in a cave. Fear makes us do irrational things. What irrational thing have you done out of fear? We can turn to God and trust Him when we are overtaken by fear or ask for His help in fearful surroundings. Just call His name out loud, and God will come running for His beloved. Become fearless in calling out His name.

Day 78: Read 1 Samuel 23:1-6
David's men were afraid.

David inquired of the Lord not once but twice, and didn't make a move without His guidance. After David's men said they were afraid, he encouraged them by giving them God's direction. Attaining God's will beforehand is so important. If not, we often have to learn hard lessons for not following God's will. When have you sought God's guidance first? When have you gone ahead of Him? Take time to discern God's will in all areas of your life. God communicates with us through time spent reading the Bible, through counseling words from others, and through the guidance of the Holy Spirit. Be patient, and don't make a move without His guidance. Become fearless in seeking God's will.

Day 79: Read 1 Samuel 23:7-29
Jonathan encouraged David; do not be afraid.

When David learned that Saul had come after him to take his life, he was frightened. His friend Jonathan encouraged him and reminded him what God has already done for him. Before this day, God had already united Jonathan and David in a solid friendship. They had immediately confided, trusted, and loved one another with agapé love. The Lord gives us these special and meaningful relationships. In times of trouble, who has helped you find and gain your strength again? Strengthening and investing in deep meaningful friendships are pleasing to God, who asks us to love others as our self. Become fearless in seeking friendships from God.

Day 80: Read 1 Samuel 28:1-25
The king told her not to be afraid.

Saul had already disobeyed God once, but he made his rebellion even worse by seeking help from the occult. God is very clear throughout His Word that He is against witchcraft, mediums, and anyone who consults with or conjures up the dead. In Saul's desperation for answers, he sought advice from a medium. When the witch of Endor saw the great power of God, she feared greatly because she was used to seeing demonic forces that were not as great as God. The message was clear that the demise of Saul and his sons were near. Have you ever sought answers to your problems from sources other than the Lord? Remember God communicates with us in clear channels—the Bible, the Holy Spirit, and godly, mature Christians. Become fearless in always seeking these channels.

2 SAMUEL

Day 81: Read 2 Samuel 1:1-16
David asked the Amalekite why he was not afraid to destroy the Lord's anointed.

All authority belongs to God, who appoints and anoints those He sees fit. We may not understand the reasons, but we must respect God. God appointed Saul as king, and God was the only One to remove him from that office. Even though Saul sought to kill David on more than one occasion, David remained respectful and put aside his hurt and anger. He knew God was with him and does everything for a reason. We believers have a hard time understanding why someone wouldn't be afraid of God and argue against the one He appointed. How do you maintain friendships in difference of opinion or political turmoil? Political opinions over positions of power have plagued friendships and families forever; love them anyway just like Jesus loves you! Don't allow any issue to get in the way of loving each other. Focus on the good and positive and let the rest go. Become fearless in loving others with different opinions.

Day 82: Read 2 Samuel 9:1-13
Do not be afraid; I will show you kindness.

David made a covenant with his beloved friend, Jonathan, to always show kindness to his descendants. David was a leader of integrity and called for Jonathan's son, Mephibosheth, to appear before him. Mephibosheth, a known enemy, was fearful to appear before King David. He bowed down to the king, and David showed him compassion and cared for him— as he promised he would. Have you ever been shown compassion by others when you didn't deserve it? God shows His compassion for us every day, and we don't deserve it. Become fearless in compassion.

Day 83: Read 2 Samuel 10:1-19
The Arameans were afraid to help Hanun and the Ammonites anymore.

If you waste your time and energy looking for the bad in people, you may find it like Hanun did. Hanun sought the opinion and advice of men instead of God. David sought God's advice and knew He would do what was right for them. God gave David a victory that caused Hanun to lose all of his other alliances. Do you accept people at face value and assume they are good people or are you cautious, thinking they possibly have ulterior motives? Even if they did, after a few moments of talking with you and witnessing the goodness of Jesus in your words, perhaps they would change their tune. Look for the positive in people. Expect God to do what is right in His sight. Become fearless in seeking the good in people.

Day 84: Read 2 Samuel 14:1-33
I will speak boldly for a second chance because the people have made me afraid.

David failed to teach his children the way of the Lord. His son, Absalom, was a sinful and rebellious man who facilitated the murder of his own half-brother and escaped for fear of the people. Years later, a woman successfully petitioned the king on Absalom's behalf. The king saw the resemblance of her story and his own and allowed Absalom to return home. The king granted Absalom a second chance. The Father always grants His children a second chance. Children need discipline and second chances to prove what they have learned. God gives us second chances to do better and to become a thriving part of His kingdom. How many chances has God given you? Live, learn, and grow stronger from them. Be who God created you to be. Become fearless in successfully living out second chances.

58

Day 85: Read 2 Samuel 17:1-29
The bravest soldier, whose heart is like a lion, will melt in fear of your father.

David's son Absalom listened to bad advice and went to war against his own father, the king. His first mistake was inquiring of others instead of God. Attacking David when he was weak and weary was Absalom's second mistake. David and his men were experienced warriors with brave hearts like those of lions. The advice Absalom received was false encouragement, flattery, and predicted glory if he led his troops into battle. He chose his own pride and glory over possible destruction. Have you ever been falsely encouraged? God is the great Encourager; seek His counsel. Gain the heart of a lion! Become fearless in seeking God's advice.

Day 86: Read 2 Samuel 23:1-7
One will rule over men in righteousness and in the fear of God.

In David's last words, he prophesied about the return of Jesus, the great and perfect ruler. Although he did not know when the Savior would return, He encouraged his men to live right and keep their houses in order. No one knows the day or hour that Jesus will return, so we should live today like it may be our last. Is your house in order? Prepare for the day that your salvation will come to fruition. Become fearless in the reality of Jesus' return.

1 KINGS

Day 87: Read 1 Kings 1:1-53
From his own failed deception, Adonijah became fearful and afraid of the new king.

Before Solomon was pronounced king, his brother, Adonijah, schemed to take the royal seat. When his ploy failed, he became fearful and afraid of King Solomon. Adonijah turned and ran to the altar of God, seeking safety. God is a great help in all times, especially in times of trouble. But think how much better our lives would be when we seek God's will first. When have you contrived to create your own success? Put aside the schemes of selfishness and seek the blessings that God will bestow upon us. Become fearless in seeking God's will first.

Day 88: Read 1 Kings 8:22-45
All will hear your name and fear you.

When King Solomon was dedicating the Lord's temple, he prayed that all men would fear God. Since the Lord knows all the hearts of men, Solomon prayed this prayer for his men and foreigners alike. Do you pray and hope for all to hear the word of the Lord and fear Him? We believers are the living message from God. We are to spread love through the message of the gospel. A foreigner is any person who has not heard or accepted the gospel. Become fearless in praying for foreigners.

Day 89: Read 1 Kings 17:1-24
Don't be afraid; the jar of flour and jug of oil will not be used up.

Throughout the Bible, God continually provides for His people and makes resources stretch and last longer than humanly possible. When Elijah asked the widow from Zarephath to prepare a meal for him, he was asking her to give up the last meal that she and her young son would eat. She had faith that Elijah was a man of God and did as he asked. Through her faith and obedience, God allowed them all to see many miracles. God used the flour and oil over again and again, and that small amount never ran out. What has God provided for you and stretched past what is humanly possible? When we become obedient, God is the ultimate provider of every need we have. Become fearless is recognizing God as the Provider.

Day 90: Read 1 Kings 19:1-9
Elijah was afraid and ran for his life.

Elijah was feeling down and exhausted after the victories the Lord had given him. He feared he was the only faithful servant left alive and wondered what was next. The Lord cared for him, gave him rest, and restored him to continue on the path he had been given. When in fear, we can become discouraged and depressed. How does God care for you in times of fatigue, discouragement, or depression? God gives complete restoration. Become fearless in returning to His rest.

Day 91: Read 1 Kings 19:10-21
**Exhausted and discouraged, Elijah was afraid he
was the only one left who loved the Lord.**

Elijah had just experienced a great spiritual battle and triumph, but now he doubted himself. He had seen the power of God at work through him, but now he was afraid of what was next. After his great accomplishments, discouragement set in. At these times, God meets us right where we are and cares for us. God gave Elijah rest, food, then restored him and reminded him for what he had been created. Ever think you are the only one who is following after God's own heart? Even though we may not see them, many more faithful servants are also following after God's heart. You were created for a very specific purpose in God's kingdom. Become fearless in following through in your kingdom work.

2 KINGS
Day 92: Read 2 Kings 1:1-18
**The angel spoke to Elijah and told
him not to be afraid.**

As Elijah was doing God's work, ungodly King Ahaziah was seeking everything but God. Elijah listened to God and intervened with a message to remind the wayward king that God was in this place. The king dismissed the message and sent others to inquire. The third captain who came to inquire for the king had the right mindset. He humbled himself when he appeared before authority and begged for mercy. Elijah, who was committed to God, noticed the genuine attitude, and God was able to do His work on earth because of their obedience. They were fearless because God was with them. Do you have a servant's heart toward others? Work humbly together for the Lord. Become a fearless servant.

Day 93: Read 2 Kings 6:8-23
Don't be afraid, for those who are with us are more than those who are not.

Elisha's servant was no longer afraid after he saw God's great army and strength. God granted Elisha's request to blind the Arameans who came to fight them. Then, they led the Arameans right into the city, and Elisha prayed for God to open their eyes. Instead of killing them, Elisha told the king of Israel to prepare a great feast for the Arameans. When we don't always get what we want can be a blessing. Doing right when others wrong us or try to harm us in some way is often difficult. Having faith to trust God in these times makes us stronger. When have you put your trust in God? How has your faith grown? Follow Him! Become fearless in your growing faith in God.

Day 94: Read 2 Kings 10:1-36
The people were terrified of Jehu's power.

Jehu had a zeal for serving the Lord and was a man of action. God used Jehu's strengths to eliminate Baal worship. He honored God by removing the Baal worship, but He abused the authority God gave him. Jehu did not submit to God's control and took matters into his own hands for his own self-gratification. He confused his personal feelings and motives, disguising it as his faith. Have you ever used your faith for your own personal gain? When we remain under God's control, we are able to use the strengths He's given us to the best of our ability, which takes the pressure from us and places it on the only Leader who can handle it. Without God, we fall terribly short. Become fearless in using your strengths to the best of His ability.

1 CHRONICLES

Day 95: Read 1 Chronicles 12:1-22
The warriors had faces of lions and were swift as gazelles.

Stalwart warriors, who wanted to be where God was at work, joined forces with David's army. Even champions from the opposing forces joined David, recognizing he was a fierce leader and that God was with him. These dedicated warriors had perfected their God-given skills and were ready for battle. Have you ever been drawn to a worthy cause? People are drawn to the work of God. Remain brave, obedient, and determined. Become fearless and put on the face of the lion in God's army.

Day 96: Read 1 Chronicles 13:1-14
David was afraid of God's wrath.

David was singing and dancing before the Lord with all his might as he and the assembly returned the ark to Jerusalem. When the oxen carrying the ark stumbled, Uzzah reached out to steady the ark, and the Lord struck him down. God had given specific instructions on how the ark was to be moved and, in sincerity, Uzzah disobeyed. David didn't follow God's instructions; he followed instruction from others as to how the ark should be transported. Have you ever set out on your own understanding of a situation only to learn later you were wrong? Our enthusiasm for God must follow with obedience to His teachings. Understand the Bible and investing in learning God's way is important. Become fearless in understanding God's laws.

Day 97: Read 1 Chronicles 21:1-30
David was overwhelmed and afraid of the mighty and awesome power of God.

David's pride took over, and he ordered a census on the land. A tally of all the able-bodied, fighting men was prepared for him. In ordering the census, David was trusting and relying on his military strength and power instead of God. The wrath of God was mighty against David and his people. David probably felt great shame that many died for his failure of sin and disobedience. Our disobedience to God not only affects us, it affects everyone God has put into our lives. Consider how much more our *obedience* to God affects us and others. How does your sin affect others in your life? The 70,000 lives that were lost because of David's disobedience could have been changed had he been obedient to God. Put aside pride and trust God. God is counting on you to trust Him and pave the way for others into His kingdom. Become fearless in letting go of pride.

Day 98: Read 1 Chronicles 22:1-19
Be strong and courageous; do not be afraid or discouraged.

David was given orders by God that his son, Solomon, had been chosen to build the temple. When David had a conversation with his son about building the temple, he told him all the specifications for building the temple and encouraged him to be strong and courageous. He also reminded Solomon not to be afraid or discouraged for the Lord was with him and would give him success. What a powerful and memorable conversation between father and son! When have you been encouraged by another in this way? Have you encouraged others this way? When we are given encouragement, it helps us to be strong, courageous, and have no fear. Become fearless in encouraging others.

Day 99: Read 1 Chronicles 28:1-21
David reminded Solomon to be strong
and to do the work.

The day David handed over the temple plans, two times he reminded Solomon to *be strong* and to *do the work. Do the work* means "don't stray from the plan that God gave you." David reminded Solomon to stay on track, keep up, be obedient, be selfless, and ready to serve as directed. Have you ever had explicit instructions from the Lord? Did you carry out His directions to completion? God specifically created each of us for a unique purpose. Explore through prayer what your heart's desire is, then dig in, and do the work He has given you. Become fearless in working for the Lord.

2 CHRONICLES

Day 100: Read 2 Chronicles 17:1-19
The fear of the Lord fell on all the
kingdoms around Judah.

The Lord established His kingdom under Jehoshaphat because he walked in the way of the Lord, and his heart was devoted only to Him. The fear of the Lord fell on all other nations because the Lord was with the kingdom of Judah. The majority of God's people were far from Him; they didn't take the time to understand God's law. The people of Judah understood God's power so they feared Him but didn't revere or worship God. Probably many people today fear God, but they fail to revere Him. What portion of time do you devote to better know God each day? Investing precious time learning with others in Bible studies, having family devotions, and spending time alone with God is essential to revering Him. Make time for Him. Become fearless in revering God in study.

Day 101: Read 2 Chronicles 19:1-11
Let the fear of the Lord be on you as you wholeheartedly work for Him.

Jehoshaphat reminded the leaders of the standards to employ in judging the people. He warned that the fear of God would be on them and to judge the people by God's laws. The only thing we are to fear in this life is God. Being honest and following God's law starts in the household and extends into the workplace. Just as the leaders Jehoshaphat recruited as judges were held to a certain standard, we are also held to these same standards today as we work for God. Did you ever abuse your position of power and influence with others? We are not leaders for man; we are leaders for the Lord. We are to follow His rules and align our judgment to fit His. Become a fearless leader of the Lord.

Day 102: Read 2 Chronicles 20:1-30
Do not be afraid; the battle is the Lord's.

Frightened by the news that Jehoshaphat's men would be facing a great battle, he reminded them that this is the Lord's battle. The men remained calm, full of trust, and sang songs to God as they marched to the frontlines. That's faith in action! We become fearless when we trust God through our faith in Him. When have you displayed your faith in action? Through the men's singing and faithfulness, God delivered their enemies into their hands. For whatever reason God is calling you to the frontlines, step forth with a song in your heart and in a body that is fearless. God is calling you to be faithful and to trust in Him; invite God into your weaknesses. The battle is the Lord's! Become fearless in your faith by trusting God.

Day 103: Read 2 Chronicles 26:1-5
Instruction in the fear of God.

Uzziah was a man after God's own heart, and God saw his obedience and reverence to Him. When we operate our lives in obedient reverence to God, He will bless it. Uzziah feared God as he was instructed, and God gave him success. When we fear God and do right, the Lord will give us success. How can you operate your life in greater obedience to God? Lay it all at His feet and gain His strength. Become fearless in submission to Jesus.

Day 104: Read 2 Chronicles 32:1-23
Hezekiah encouraged them to be strong and courageous, and not to be afraid.

What a complete joy to be encouraged by another with the power of God! King Hezekiah had great faith and wasn't shaken by the numerous legions of the opposing army. The Lord fights our battles. We, as believers, have greater power because God is with us. When we come to God in prayer, amazing things happen. Great power rests in having God's favor. How has God's power worked in your life? God cared for Hezekiah and his people, and He will also care for you in your daily battles. Become fearless in the confidence of God's power.

EZRA

Day 105: Read Ezra 3:1-13
Despite the fear of those around them, they continued to follow God.

The children of Israel built an altar to the Lord as a place to worship and to rededicate their lives daily to God. They stood out and were doing a new thing by rebuilding the altar to the Lord. The Jewish people stood together despite their fears. They sacrificed offerings to the Lord which showed others that they daily sought after God. The fear of others' not conforming to their beliefs and trying to take their land didn't stop them from seeking, honoring, praising, and obeying God. How have others gotten in the way of your living out your life for God? Don't let the fear of what others think or act get in the way of your walk with God. No one has that kind of power over you. Become fearless in living out your love of God for all to see.

NEHEMIAH

Day 106: Read Nehemiah 2:1-10
Nehemiah was greatly afraid, but he petitioned the king anyway.

For Nehemiah to show emotional sadness before the king was dangerous. Nehemiah was emotionally overcome with the thought of his forefathers buried in ruins. He was very encouraged when God asked him to rebuild the walls of Jerusalem. Even though he was afraid of the king, he didn't allow his fear to stop him. Nehemiah recognized his fear and boldly stepped into it because He knew God was with him. What has God asked you to do that you have not done because of fear? Don't allow your fears to become bigger than God. Complete the task and give God the glory! Become fearless in walking through fear.

Day 107: Read Nehemiah 4:1-23
Don't be afraid; the Lord will fight for you.

Nehemiah strengthened the crew of workers who were growing faint, overwhelmed by the task of rebuilding the walls of Jerusalem. He reminded them they were working for God to complete a specific goal and that God would protect them from the encompassing threats. When God calls us into a specific job, ministry, or neighborhood and we are obedient, He will protect us and bless us as we serve Him. God, who is power, is also the giver of strength and power. How has God given you strength and power to complete a task? Harvest God's awesome power and push through to complete the task He's given you. Become fearless in endurance.

Day 108: Read Nehemiah 5:1-19
We should always walk in the fear of our God.

Nehemiah heard the cry of the starving people, who were mortgaging their land and selling their children into slavery. They were working hard at rebuilding the walls, but they couldn't get ahead because of unfair business practices. Some of the wealthy families were dishonoring God by becoming rich at the expense and hardship of others. God calls us then and now to be fair in business and to care for the poor among us. After the wealthy had been confronted, they worked together to care for one another and eliminate poverty. Needy people are everywhere. How do you care for the poor around you? Out of reverence to God, do for others as you would like to have done for you. Become fearless in helping the poor among you.

Day 109: Read Nehemiah 6:1-19
The enemies were afraid because they saw what the Lord can do.

When the leaders of the opposition, Sanballat and Tobiah, saw the walls were almost finished, they became desperate and attacked Nehemiah's character to stop the building. When others see our success with God's help, they attack our character by starting hurtful rumors and lies to put an end to God's work. Nehemiah didn't give them any space or power; he called out their lies, deceit, and false reports for what they were—untruths. With God's help, he continued on to successfully complete the wall. How has the Enemy attacked your character when completing a God-given task? When our enemies see the power of God, they lose their self-confidence and often stop their pursuit of us. Be straightforward and don't fall victim to the Enemy's strategy. Become fearless in calling out the opposition.

Day 110: Read Nehemiah 7:1-3
Those with integrity fear God more than most.

Nehemiah singled out Hanani and Hananiah as men of integrity and reverence to God. He gave them desirable roles in charge of Jerusalem. These qualities for leaders were important then and are equally important today. A leader with great integrity operates in both truth and is trustworthy of completing his work. God is integrity. When we revere God, we take His priorities as our own. Are you one of integrity and reverence to God in all aspects of your life? If not, on what area do you need to work? God-fearing people want to have the same priorities as God. Become fearless in fearing God more than most.

ESTHER

Day 111: Read Esther 9:1-32
No one could stand against the Jews; all others were afraid of them.

Mordecai had the king sign a new edict that allowed the Jews to fight back when and if they were attacked. This resistance surprised their enemies, and even as the Jews were defeating their enemies, Esther again risked her life by asking the king for the Jews to be able to defend themselves and fight another day. During this time period, women were expected to be quiet and not to voice their opinions. Esther was a faithful Jewish woman who became fearless to help God's people. How have you risked it all to help another? Be bold, brave, and stand out. Become fearless in helping God's people.

JOB

Day 112: Read Job 1:1-22
The blameless one feared God and shunned evil.

Satan, who is limited by God's power and can only do what God permits, set out to test one of God's faithful. When tragedy fell on Job, he grieved in worship, but he did not sin against God by charging Him with wrongdoing. He only praised, realizing the Lord, who has authority over all, gives and takes away. Job, a blameless man who fears God and shuns evil, proved Satan wrong. This test confirmed that Job loved God for what He had already done for him and had given him. How do you respond to God during testing and trials? Love God for who He is and what He's already done for you. Become fearless in loving God for who He is.

Day 113: Read Job 2:1-13
The one who fears God will accept the good from Him as well as the trouble.

Satan tested Job a second time by attacking his physical body. Job suffered with painful sores all over his body, yet even with his own wife's prompting, he did not curse God for his pain. Even though Job has now lost his children, his property, and his health to pain and suffering, he still saw God's goodness. God allows us to have bad experiences to test and strengthen our faith. God knew Job would declare God's goodness and would prove to Satan the awesome power of God. Do you question God's goodness when trouble comes your way? God is the same yesterday, today, and tomorrow. Become fearless in accepting God's goodness during troubled times.

Day 114: Read Job 3:1-26
Job's worst fear has happened.

Job who was an upright man of God, prayed, repented of his sins, and loved God. He was so miserable from the physical pain and suffering while mourning the deaths of his children, he cursed the day he was born. He never cursed God—only his birth. All of his right living was crumbling before him. Has your life come crumbling down before you even though you were living right in God's Word? God's love doesn't prevent us from experiencing trials and suffering. Sometimes bad things do happen to good people. God's love is bigger than anything we will ever face. Keep loving Him. Become fearless in letting nothing separate you from the love of God.

Day 115: Read Job 5:1-27
You will be protected and need not fear when the time of destruction comes.

Job's friends assumed that his suffering was because of some great sin he had committed against God; his sins were the reason for his suffering. Blaming a person for the trials that come in his life is easy, but God asks us to be free from this kind of thinking. Remember that God made the good times as well as the bad. It's not *if* the time of destruction comes, it's *when* the time of destruction comes. God will use those trials and hard times of life to grow and strengthen us through them. Have you ever judged people because of the trials they were facing? Don't assume we know the truth about a life we have never lived. Remember that, as believers, our lives are protected through eternity. Become fearless *when* the time of destruction comes.

Day 116: Read Job 6:1-30
One in trouble should have the devotion of his friends—even if he abandons the fear of God.

Job, who always tried to live right was overwhelmed when his friends assumed he had sinned against God. His friends were afraid of what they saw and were of no help to him. In fact, they made matters worse with their judgments. Job believed his integrity was at stake because he was not guilty of sin as his friends claimed. Have you ever made a situation worse by *trying* to help a friend? Friendships are important to God, and throughout Scripture, He asks us to love and care for one another. Life is a team sport; don't leave anyone behind. Become fearless in never leaving behind a friend.

Day 117: Read Job 11:1-20
Devote your heart to God, then you will stand firm without fear.

Zophar, the last of Job's friends to speak had the harshest words. He also insisted Job's suffering was due to the sins he had committed against God. Zophar called Job deceitful and even lectured him about how to live right. Zophar told Job to confess his sins, devote his heart to God, and then he would stand firm without fear. That advice is good and true for many people, but his opinion wasn't true of Job, who was blameless before the Lord. When have you tried to help others without inquiring of the Lord first? When we run ahead of God to help others, sometimes we make matters worse and hurt others with our words. Make sure your own heart is devoted to God before helping others and seek Him first. Become fearless in devoting your own heart to God.

Day 118: Read Job 19:1-29
You should fear the judgment of God for the wrath will be punished.

Even through it all, Job maintains his faith and boasts that his Redeemer lives, and he will one day see Him. He reminded his friends that judgment would come, and God will certainly punish the anger displayed against him. Job's faith was so strong, he knew that God would punish evil and reward virtue. Do you speak words of anger or have anger in your heart for another? God sees everything and hears every unsaid thought. Remember we will stand before Him and give an account for the life we lived. Live one of love—not hate. Become fearless in awaiting judgment.

Day 119: Read Job 21:1-34
Some are safe and free from fear, yet they are far from God.

Job argues that sinful people who do not fear God can live well and experience success. Sinners may experience wealth, but their abundance will run out. Their time on earth has an ending, and they will have to give an answer for how they used their resources and gifts from God. Job's friends viewed success from an outward appearance. God doesn't look at your accomplishments or failures; He looks at your heart. How hard are you on yourself in viewing your failures and attaining success? Invest in yourself, spend time with God, and let Him be the achievement in your life. Become fearless in having a successful heart for God.

Day 120: Read Job 23:1-17
No one can oppose God that is why we fear Him.

Job feared God because He was, above all, the most powerful being. He told his friends that God is above all; no one can compete against Him. Job also told them he was a man of integrity and walked in obedience to God's laws. He was distraught and desperately wanted to know the reasons for his suffering. Through his trials and testing, Job had not lost his faith in God. How do you keep your faith when you don't have answers for your sufferings? Above all, fear God, keep going, and don't stop! Become fearless in sincere faith of God.

Day 121: Read Job 28:1-28
It is wise to fear the Lord and shun evil.

Job stated to his friends that wisdom doesn't dwell here on earth among the living. To fear the Lord is wisdom and to shun evil is understanding God. Often we place a high regard on our religious leaders, allowing them to teach us everything we need to know about God. We need to remember they're just people too. People make mistakes; God doesn't. Go right to the source who supplies your wisdom and understanding—God. Spend time with Him reading the Bible and allow Him to fill your willing spirit with His love and knowledge of how to live and treat others. Having a one-on-one relationship with Jesus Christ through prayer and Bible study will bestow wisdom on you. When do you meet daily with the Lord? Make wisdom part of your life and let God build your foundation in Him. Become fearless in opening up your Bible and yourself to God.

Day 122: Read Job 31:1-40
For fear of His splendor, I could not sin.

Job scanned his life and stated the sins he had not committed and the deeds he insisted on upholding. He declared the reason he could not commit sins against God was because of God's glory. The magnificence of God kept Job from sinning and spurred him on to live upright before the Lord. Do you view God the way Job does? God leaves His believers full of awe and wonder, daydreaming about His greatness. We should fear not having the greatness of God in our lives. Stay obedient to Him and scan your life to see if there's room for His splendor. Become fearless in making room for the splendor of God.

Day 123: Read Job 32:1-22
I was fearful to tell you what I know because
my years were younger than yours.

Elihu was afraid to speak to Job because he was younger than the rest of Job's friends. Assuming God can't use those who are younger than we are means missing out on great lessons from Him. God uses everyone at every age in life to do His will. We should not have fear at any age to share our opinions, values, and strengths with others. God created us all for such a time as this. Have you ever denounced someone because of their age, made a playful but possibly hurtful joke, or decided in your heart that a person was too young to consider? We believers need to change our actions and also our way of thinking about God's kingdom. With age comes wisdom, but no one knows whose age is the wisest. Everyone whose walk is in the Lord gains wisdom each day they seek Him. Stand firm and be courageous in the Lord. Become fearless in speaking for God.

Day 124: Read Job 33:1-33
No fear of me or my words should alarm you.

Elihu thought Job wasn't listening to God about why he was suffering. He told Job how God speaks to us though dreams, visions, and angels, but Job already knew that. What Elihu didn't know was that Job was experiencing the biggest testing of his life. Job's test was to trust in God even when he didn't understand what was going on or have the answers from Him. The words of Elihu were uninformed about God, and Job did not fear them. If God would have answered Job's question, he wouldn't have gained strength and wisdom from the testing. What questions do you have for God that still remain unanswered? Invite God into that pain and trust Him as He shows you the way—even if it's silent. Become fearless in trusting God even when you don't understand.

Day 125: Read Job 37:1-24
**Wise-hearted men revere God because of the
mighty and majestic roar of His voice.**

Elihu described how nothing can compare to the marvelous ways of the Lord. He went on to implore fellow believers to really "*Listen!*" Listen to the roar of God's voice and hear Him when He speaks. Having faith by waiting for God is more desirable than having all the answers to our problems. God will speak when He is ready. How do you hear God when He speaks to you? Search for Him in prayer, reading the Bible, the Holy Spirit, dreams and visions. When you revere God and search for Him, you will find Him. Become fearless in listening for the roar of God.

Day 126: Read Job 40:1-24 and 41:1-34
**The Lord speaks, and nothing equals the
power of God who is without fear.**

God answered Job with multiple questions—so many of them that Job had no clue how to answer. God showed Job that He had all knowledge and had created everything, even the things Job hadn't yet considered. Nothing equals the power of God; He controls all forces of nature. God knew Job couldn't answer His questions; He only wanted Job to see His awesome power and submit to Him. Then Job could hear God's answer for him. Waiting for the Lord to speak is hard, but so worth the wait! When He speaks, we get a glimpse of pure heaven. What is it like when God speaks to you? God, who is without fear, asks us believers to enter into His power. Give God time to reveal His answer to you; His timing not yours. Become fearless in knowing why we wait on God to answer.

PSALMS

Day 127: Read Psalm 2:1-12
Serve the Lord with fear and trembling, for time is short.

David described a rebellious people and the coming of Christ—the time of God's ultimate rule. Everybody eventually serves something in one way or another. Some serve false religions or their own selfish desires. We are free to choose what or who we will serve, but keep in mind that our service will run out along with our time on earth. What or who do you wholeheartedly serve? We don't need to fear those who don't serve God. We only need to focus on our own surrender to Him. Submit and prepare for His return. Make straight paths for the Lord. Become fearless in His service.

Day 128: Read Psalm 3:1-8
I will not fear those who attack me on all sides; God will deliver me.

David was literally under attack on all sides. Tens of thousands of enemies were drawing near to attack and take over. He cried out to God and depended on His mercy—not on his own troops. David knew God would deliver him from all the enemies. When we are under attack by crisis or turmoil, the Lord is our only refuge. God is the author of protection and the giver of peace. He alone calms the storms of this life. Is God the first One you go to in times of trouble? He may send others to you to comfort, protect, and care for you in your times of need, but He needs to be your first call. He knows you better than anyone else and is watching out for you. Become fearless in seeking Him to fight your battles.

Day 129: Read Psalm 15:1-5
Those who fear the Lord will
never be shaken.

David the psalmist recaps God's standards for living. He reminds us that we live in a world full of vile evils, but if we remain true to our covenant with God, we will never be shaken. Even though we live among others whose moral standards aren't like ours, we believers need to keep our oath to God. Our oath should not slander or blaspheme anyone. How do you honor God with your words? Keep your promise to the Lord and let nothing shake you! Become fearless in the oath you made to God.

Day 130: Read Psalm 16:1-11
The Lord is always before me;
I will not be shaken.

Through constant communication, David allows God to lead him in the way which he should go. The Lord always goes before him. Because David follows after God, he will not be shaken by anything that comes his way. David knew that his companionship with God was a secure relationship built on trust. Have you ever falsely placed your security? Confidently place your security in the companionship of Jesus. Live according to what is right in His eyes. Become fearless in your security in Jesus Christ.

Day 131: Read Psalm 19:1-14
The fear of the Lord is pure.

The law of the Lord is perfect and so is the fear. God created fear to warn of danger and to guide our lives away from the danger. His laws also revive our souls and give us joy. Have you ever felt like you cannot live up to God's laws, aren't good enough, or have unknowingly sinned against them? Remember His laws are to protect, revive, warn, and bring joy—not make us feel guilty or unworthy. Become fearless living in God's laws.

Day 132: Read Psalm 21:1-13
Through unfailing love, he will not be shaken.

David recognized and thanked God for giving him great success and answered prayers. In battle, David trusted in God, who provided him stable ground; therefore, he couldn't be shaken. We cannot be shaken on the solid and stable grounds of God. Neither can we be shaken from God's favor because He loves us unconditionally. Unfailing love never quits. In who or what do you wrongfully place your trust? God never quits us; never quit Him. Become fearless in your love for God.

Day 133: Read Psalm 22:1-31
All who fear the Lord, praise Him.

David wrote about his suffering, sorrow, and deeply felt pain of rejection. He felt despised by others around him. When David cried out to God with his pain, God heard him and gave him strength. Then David publically praised God. He wanted all to know the greatness that is God. Have you praised God in public, taken the stage at church to profess how God has worked in your life, or taken to social media to share a blessing from God? Praise Him publically so the next generation can see and learn. Become fearless today in proclaiming the goodness that is God.

Day 134: Read Psalm 23:1-6
I walk through the valley of death,
I will fear no evil.

David beautifully describes how the Lord guides and provided for his needs. He calls the Lord his Shepherd. A *shepherd* is "a guide or a leader." When we view the Lord as our Good Shepherd and follow His lead, we will have no fear in death because we will be comforted and cared for. The Lord went ahead of us and prepared a table for us. Do you have a reservation at the Lord's eternal banquet? Death isn't permanent. Become fearless in dwelling in the house of the Lord forever.

Day 135: Read Psalm 25:1-22
The Lord confides in the ones who fear Him.

In David's prayer for defense, he clearly states the truths and understanding of his relationship with God. He knows his own weaknesses and how much he needs God. David trusts that God will be with him and confide in him because he fears the Lord. Do you view Jesus as a friend with whom you can confide anything? Jesus wants to know and hear everything about you—even the things you've deemed too silly to chat about. Give yourself completely over to God; He can't wait to hear your voice. Become fearless in your friendship with Jesus.

Day 135: Leap Year: Read Psalm 27:1-14
The Lord is my light, whom shall I fear or be afraid?

David describes fear as a darkness that holds us captive. Nothing is more powerful than God, and nothing should take away our attention from Him. David rid himself of fear by realizing the Lord is the light in the darkness and the giver of salvation. We can also rid ourselves of fear by calling on the name of the Lord when fear creeps in. What fear still holds you captive? When the darkness of fear sets in, quickly remember the Lord is the Light of our salvation. Fear has no chance! Become fearless to fear less.

Day 136: Read Psalm 33:1-22
**Let everyone on earth fear the Lord
and revere Him.**

What a beautiful day it will be when all people on earth will fear and submit to the Lord! Everyone will praise in submission and reverence to our Creator—not only because of what He can do but for His unfailing love. God is with those believers who love, honor, and fear Him as Lord of all. We can place our hope and trust in Him. How many friends or family do you have who fear the Lord and believe in Him? Oftentimes the number of our friends who don't fear God outnumber the ones who do. You're not alone; it's time for a revival to grow strong in numbers! Become fearless in seeking like-minded believers.

Day 137: Read Psalm 34:1-22
Fear the Lord and lack nothing.

David praised God for always being there for him. God always hears our prayers and acts on our behalf when we need Him. Through obedience and prayer, He removes our fears and shows us kindness. Do you fear God? To fear Him is to show respect and honor in all of life's situations—not only when it is fitting for you. We remain humble through our fear of God and lack nothing. God is more than enough. Become fearless in lacking nothing.

Day 138: Read Psalm 36:1-12
There is no fear of God.

For those who knowingly sin, there is no fear of God. When there is no fear of God, people enjoy conflict, their actions are evil, their words are deceitful, and they don't reject what is wrong. Who do you know like this in your life? God is just and will not let them go unpunished—no matter what they've done. We do not fear evil people because God will judge them, and they will answer to Him. We believers fear God only because He loves us, provides for us, and will gather us to Him in eternity. Become fearless in the reverence to God.

Day 139: Read Psalm 40:1-17
For those who wait patiently, they will see, fear, and put their trust in the Lord.

God blessed David after he waited patiently on the Lord. He heard David's cry, lifted him out of his despair, gave him a firm foundation on which to stand, and put a new song in his heart. If David didn't wait patiently, he would have forfeited all these blessings from God. A lot can be done while we wait patiently on the Lord. Oftentimes we become paralyzed and immobile with fear in the wait because the outcome we expected or anticipated isn't happening in our time frame or at all. What blessings have you been given after waiting on the Lord? While you wait, keep moving! The wait will not change your love for God. Adjust your outlook, keep serving others, and love God while you wait. Your blessings and lessons will be bestowed on you after enduring the trial of the wait. Trust that God's got you! Become fearless in the wait.

Day 140: Read Psalm 46:1-11
We will not fear even when the earth gives way.

God is our present-day refuge and strength. Getting to know Him in the present day helps us prepare for the final days. God is in control, and He saves those who love Him. God's faithful believers will not be fearful when the earth gives way to the mountains which fall to the sea and neither will they fear the roaring waters. The believers will be at peace because of their confidence in the eternal God. Will you be still now, spend time with Him, and know Him? When war and destruction overcome the earth, we not fear because God has overcome the world! Become fearless in the end times.

Day141: Read Psalm 49:1-20
Have no fear when days of evil come.

When we die, we cannot take our possessions with us. The poor and the rich appear before the Lord the same awaiting judgment. When we live by the Word of God, we have no fear when days of evil come. Evil days are already happening today when the world promotes wealth, financial gain, and most place their trust in wealth. You can't take it with you! How do you share of your wealth or lack of wealth with others? We the believers who have accepted Jesus are wealthier than most! Become fearless in using resources for kingdom work.

Day 142: Read Psalm 52:1-9
All the righteous believers will see and fear.

David wrote this psalm after being betrayed by one who had appeared to be a loyal warrior. We have all known someone who looks good on the outside but is not one of stellar character. Mistaking success and strength for goodness is easy. People aren't always successful because they've done things right and pleasing to God. We righteous believers see through this, fear the Lord, and lament their demise. Our goal is to let God reign in all that we do. Where in your life could you become more honorable in your actions? Become righteous from the inside out by comparing your actions to the Word of God. Become fearless in living out the Word of God.

Day 143: Read Psalm 54:1-7
It appears evil is without fear, but all mankind will fear God.

David cried out to God telling Him all about the conspiracies of evil against him. Evil comes in both spiritual and physical forms. The attack of words or pain and suffering often come when we least expect it. Satan loves to catch us off guard and attack us when we are at our weakest. Have you ever felt like David and cried out to God for His help? God knows everything that happens to us in every form of evil. He has already won the battle over evil. The victory was already won! Become fearless in crying out to God.

Day 144: Read Psalm 55:1-15
In my anguish, fear and trembling
have overwhelmed me.

David expressed his bereaved heart resulting from the betrayal of a friendship. He cried out to God with his broken heart and asked God to help through constant prayer. David prayed to God faithfully throughout his day. Friends are often the ones who can hurt us the most. Sometimes the hurt is done on purpose and sometimes unintentionally. Do you take your broken heart to God in times of trouble? God is the only One who can heal our broken hearts. He takes out the hurt and fills it with His love. He is the great Comforter. Bring your bereaved heart to Him. Become fearless in seeking God as your Comforter.

Day 145: Read Psalm 55:16-23
Those who never change their ways
have no fear of God.

David experienced great distress and grief over the death of his son, Absalom. His death was at the hand of his own men because of Absalom's rebellion. Betrayal is tough to experience especially by your loved ones, friends, and family. Godly friendships are ones built on trust, compassion, encouragement, forgiveness, and the willingness to change for the better. What kind of friend are you? Practice godly traits and turn into the type of friend you seek. Become fearless in godly friendships.

Day 146: Read Psalm 56:1-13
When I am afraid, I will trust in the Lord.

David was under attack and fleeing for safety. He put his trust in the Lord and gained peace. This psalm reminds us that we may suffer in this life at the hands of people who will hurt us physically and mentally, but God has the final word. His believers will live on. Do you trust the Lord with your life? God knows every hurt and pain that happens to us. Have faith and trust in God over our fears. Become fearless in faith over fears.

Day 147: Read Psalm 57:1-11
I am among the lions whose tongues are like sharp swords.

David was wise for taking his troubles directly to the Lord. He cried out to God about those who were persecuting him and making his life miserable. When we are in times of trouble and are persecuted by liars, gossips, and slanderers, we don't need to retaliate with words. We need to take our trouble to the Lord who works on our behalf, taking our turmoil and giving us peace and strength. Our battles aren't against man; they're against the evil that is within man. This is God's territory. David poured out his heart to God, and God gave him peace to face another day. Do you seek the Lord in times of trouble or do you retaliate? Become fearless in not fighting in God's territory.

Day 148: Read Psalm 60:1-12
**You have raised a banner for
those who fear you.**

We, the believers, are never alone. When it feels like God is far away, remember He is always in control. God may use rejection and stillness as teaching and correction to bring you back to Him in repentance. When the world seems out of control, we need only to remember who has created and sustains it. In your relationship with God, how has He used quietness and rejection to bring you to repentance? Remember you are never alone even in quiet times. God has a plan for you and wants you to seek Him. Become fearless in seeking God's help.

Day 149: Read Psalm 62:1-12
**God is our hope and salvation;
we will not be shaken.**

David beautifully described how he placed all of his hope in the salvation of the Lord. He is resting in God alone; and in God's strength, nothing can shake him. David, as usual, poured out his heart to God in prayer. When we do this, it invites God and all that He is to help us. Even when God helps us with our problems, rest assured more are on the way. How do you deal with the daily problems, struggles, and stresses of this life? Our hope comes daily from the Lord—one prayer at a time and one blessing at a time. The waiting and the relaxing in the salvation of God is our hope that cannot be shaken. We, the believers of Jesus Christ, will not be shaken! Become fearless in the hope of your salvation.

Day 150: Read Psalm 64:1-10
Evil lives without fear today, but in the end all mankind will fear God.

Those who do not fear God can be ruthless in the pursuit of the innocent. David was under attack and being pursued by evil. He took refuge in God who is the great protector from all evil. We believers praise God in the trials and the storms of our lives because He has gone before us, knows the way, and sees our hurts and pains. When you see evil conspiring against you or your loved ones, how do you handle it? Cry out and tell God all your needs. Take heart, knowing that God will turn evil's own tongue against him. Become fearless in taking refuge in God.

Day 151: Read Psalm 65:1-13
Those living far away fear the great wonders of God.

God answers prayers and provides generously for His believers. David praised God for all the wondrous blessings he had received through nature, including the great rains and harvest. He also praised God and was grateful for repentance and forgiveness of sins. God blesses us and gives us more than we need so we can share and bless others. How do you share the great blessings God has given you? Become fearless in becoming generous to others.

Day 152: Read Psalm 66:1-20
Listen to the story of those who fear God.

Nothing is more inspiring than hearing what God has done in the lives of others. Hearing other believers share their testimonies rejuvenates our spirits and stretches our gratitude to God even further. We cannot revitalize others while we still hang on to some of our sins. God heard the psalm writer's prayer because he continually confessed his sins to God and didn't hold on to or relish any of his sins. Do you have any sins in your life that you overlook and hold tightly? God-fearing believers don't sell themselves short; they sell out for God. Hold nothing back! Become fearless in selling out for God.

Day 153: Read Psalm 67:1-7
God's ways will be known on earth and the whole world will fear Him.

God loves the world and created everything in it, including every nation of people. God's way has become known through His believers' spreading the good news about salvation through Jesus Christ. His ways will be known by all, and then the whole world will fear Him. How does God use you to make Him known to all who are near you? May everyone we come near see Jesus in us—whether in conversation or through acts of love. God will bless us and make His face shine upon us. Become fearless in making God known.

Day 154: Read Psalm 76:1-12
God alone is to be feared.

God's power is great, and He alone is to be feared. No one can stand against Him. We can harvest God's power by making commitments to Him through faith. Make a vow to the Lord and He will give you strength to carry through. What promises have you made to God? Proclaim His goodness through commitment and gain His strength to follow through. Become fearless in your commitment to God.

Day 155: Read Psalm 85:1-13
Salvation is found in those who fear Him.

God is the Creator and Restorer of all. When we are running on empty, we need only to seek Him first, and ask for His love and joy to be poured out on us. God is able to restore people and places. He is the giver of life and the only One to fear. How has God restored you or your church? Ask God to intervene in your life and restore the places and parts that are lacking His presence. Ask Him to renew your love for Him. He will make you new! Become fearless in His restoration.

Day 156: Read Psalm 86:1-17
**Teach me your ways, Lord, that I may
always fear your name.**

David, the psalmist, deeply loved God and cried out to Him in
times of trouble. Because of David's great love for God, he
trusted Him with everything. David prayed to God and waited
for Him to answer prayers. He wanted to know everything
about God and couldn't imagine not knowing or fearing His
great name. Do you have the kind of love for God that David
describes? Spend time in prayer and kindle that reverent love
for God and His great name. Become fearless in completely
loving God.

Day 157: Read Psalm 89:1-18
God is greatly feared in heaven and on earth.

This psalm by Ethan declares that the holy ones fear God
greatly, and God is more awesome than anything in their
surroundings. The *holy ones* are God's angels, and that's quite
a statement full of love and admiration. Even in heaven, God
is to be praised and feared. Have you allowed something more
powerful than God to occupy your heart, mind, or soul? Lift
God high, and let Him become more awesome than anything
in your surroundings. Become fearless in knowing His
awesomeness.

Day 158: Read Psalm 90:1-17
Your wrath is as great as the fear of you.

Here we are reminded again to fear God, and we are urged to live a life that matters to Him. God is counting on our fear of Him to inspire us to accomplish His plan for our life. In accordance with God's plan for our life, what do you want to accomplish before it's too late? Your days are numbered and fleeting. Make your work count today. Become fearless in accomplishing your God-given plan.

Day 159: Read Psalm 91:1-16
With God, you will not fear the
terror of night or day.

When we are fearful, we are reminded that God is our great shelter and Protector. He is the One to whom we can turn when we are afraid. We can place our complete trust in God who will protect us from our fears, day or night. To turn to God and rest in His safety daily should be our highest priority. Do you dwell with God daily for safety from fears? Set a time and a place to meet Him daily. You won't want to miss it! Become fearless in seeking His safety.

Day 160: Read Psalm 96:1-13
Above all God is to be feared, and He alone, is worthy of praise.

This psalm is full of beautiful imagery of what praise and worshipping God really looks like. Praise is an all-or-nothing extravaganza displayed before the Lord. Praise and worship is always on the mind of the believer. We want our lives and all that we do to point back to Jesus. Do you have this kind of desire to worship God? Become bold in all that He has done for you, and let that gratitude build up in your heart to release it in praise! Become fearless in worshipping God for all to see.

Day 161: Read Psalm 102:1-28
Everyone on earth will fear the name of the Lord.

In times of distress, the psalmist is explaining his deep sorrows, but through it all, he knows God will remain the same and keep His promises. In our admitted weaknesses God's strengths are revealed to us. God is the same from generation to generation, and those who fear, trust, and believe in Him will receive His glory. Which weaknesses have you admitted to God? Give God the self-confessed opportunity to reveal His strengths in you. Become fearless in your weakness.

Day 162: Read Psalm 103:1-22
God crowns those who fear Him
with love and compassion.

The way God forgives and forgets our sins is something to be admired and strive for in our daily lives. God is the ultimate role model. For those who revere God and fear Him in His holiness, He forgives their confessed sins committed against Him. He removes them as far as the east is from the west. As believers, we need to forgive those who have committed sins against us and forget them. Dwelling on others' wrongdoings takes up precious space that Jesus could be filling. With whom in your life have you not made peace? Write a letter to the person, living or deceased—it doesn't matter. Do the work to live in the freedom of forgiveness. Forgive, forget, and empty out all of the old to be filled with love of Jesus. Let nothing stop you from living in the freedom of forgiveness. Become fearless in forgiving others.

Day 163: Read Psalm 112:1-10
Blessed is the man who fears the Lord,
for he has no fear of bad news.

One who fears God obeys His commands and finds true enjoyment in following God's laws. A reverent believer is gifted with God's blessings such as prosperity and freedom from fear. Receiving bad news is inevitable. Even when learning of bad news, the believer trusts God with absolutely everything. How do you fare when learning of bad news? Trust God to care for the matter completely. Relax in the relationship you've built with God, trusting He is there in good times and bad. Become fearless in hearing bad news.

Day 164: Read Psalm 118:1-29
There is nothing that man can do to me; the Lord is with me, and I will not be afraid.

The world changes around us multiple times daily, but we have security in God's unchanging love. Nothing anyone can do to us can take away the confident love that we believers have in Jesus. His love endures forever and through any situation in life. God's love is stability in an unpredictable world. When the world changes around you and you feel like you have nothing left about which to praise, tell Jesus all about it. He can't wait to hear from you. What was your last honest prayer to God about? Place your confidence in Jesus as your unchanging reliable Guide for life. Become fearless in the confident, enduring, forever love of God.

Day 165: Read Psalm 119:33-48
Fulfil your promise through me, so others will see, and the Lord will be feared.

When we commit our lives to God and submit to His will, we're granted freedom to become the people He created us to be. God's will is done on earth through us. We believers are free from sin's hold on us. When we spend time with God by reading His Word, talking and praying with Him, we are granted His peace and forgiveness from sins. Seeing God at work through another is powerful. Have you witnessed the power of God at work through someone or even yourself? Be willing to serve God and let others see His royal power. Become fearless in fulfilling His promise through you.

Day 166: Read Psalm 119:57-64
I call *friend* to all those who fear the Lord
and follow His teachings.

The saying *"You've got a friend in Jesus"* is true. Like-minded people flock together, and it's also true with the believers of Jesus Christ. Being around others who love Jesus and follow His teachings is biblical. Hebrews 10:24 and 25 tells us not to give up meeting together and to spur on one another in love. There are many believers all scattered throughout this world. Where do you like to gather with other Jesus people? Become an open hand and an outstretched arm for those you call *friend*. Become fearless in gathering with all *friends*.

Day 167: Read Psalm 119:113-120
I love your law and fear only you, God.

Double-minded people are those who haven't quite decided what they believe about God. They often try to argue with believers or make them doubt God. One of the best ways to combat the double-minded person is to ask him or her to prove their theories by reading the Bible as a reference. Once the person opens the Bible to read, God's laws will be revealed, and hopefully the person's heart and peace will be restored. The Bible, which is our guide to navigate through life, reminds us that kindness and love win every time. Do you tremble before Him in awe of His laws? Don't be lukewarm; either be hot or cold—preferably hot and on fire for the Lord. When the believer finally understands who God really is, then the flesh will tremble in fear and awe of Him. Become fearless in being single-minded for God.

Day 168: Read Psalm 128:1-6
**Those who fear God, and walk in His ways,
will be truly blessed.**

To fear the Lord is one thing, but to also walk in His ways is a true blessing—a reward that one will enjoy throughout life. When we're living right with God, our family life will benefit as the blessings flow from following God. Is your family dinner table a glimpse of the characteristics of God (peace, patience, love, joy, kindness, goodness, faithfulness, gentleness, and self-control), or do you need to improve your walk in His ways? To learn His ways, we've got to spend time with Him reading His Word. Put Him on your daily schedule. Make time to learn His ways and let Him bless you. Become fearless in reading the Word of God.

Day 169: Read Psalm 130:1-8
**Because of His unfailing love and great
forgiveness, God alone is to be feared.**

Taking time to talk to God keeps the lines of communication open. We can tell Him anything, and He can't wait to hear from us. He wants to hear the good things about you and to rejoice over you; He also wants to hear the bad with your confession of sins. Keep the door of communication open; let nothing come between your relationship with God. He forgives us every time we ask for it. That's a powerful, loving, and compassionate God Who is worthy of our love and fear. What are you holding back from God? God holds nothing against us; let's hold nothing back. Become fearless in holding nothing back.

Day 170: Read Psalm 139:1-24
**I am fearfully and wonderfully
made by God.**

God creates every one of us. He knows us before we are born.
We spent time with God before meeting anyone else in our
life. Right from the beginning, God was first in our life. He
knows everything about us—even our thoughts before we
think them. Have you ever tried to hide something from God?
He is all-knowing and always with us. Tell Him everything.
Become fearless in communication with God.

Day 171: Read Psalm 145:1-21
**God saves, hears, and answers the cries
of those who fear Him in truth.**

The Lord lifts those who fall down or bow down to Him in
reverence. He hears our joys as well as every tearful cry to
Him. He is the awesome God of compassion who is full of
splendor and majesty. He cannot wait to restore you by
hearing and answering your cries. Have you ever fallen and
not asked God to pick you up? Sure, you can stand again on
your own, but you can stand taller with God's help. Cry out to
Him and let Him lift you high. Become fearless in letting Him
lift you up.

Day 172: Read Psalm 147:1-20
**The Lord rejoices over us when we fear Him
and trust in His unfailing love.**

God genuinely loves when we trust and worship Him. When
we do, He takes care of our every need, binds our broken
hearts, blesses us with His presence, and provides for us. The
Lord rejoices when we put our hope in His unfailing love and
use the gifts He's given us. God loves us enough to give us
special skills or gifts to use in serving Him. What are your
God-given gifts? Out of reverence to God, we need to use the
skills with which He's gifted us to serve Him. These gifts are
of no use to God if not used in reverence to Him. God is the
ultimate Gift giver. Become fearless in refining His gifts.

PROVERBS

Day 173: Read Proverbs 1:1-7
To fear the Lord is to have knowledge.

The book of Proverbs, which was written by Solomon, the
wisest servant in the Bible, is full of wisdom designed to
encourage believers. Each verse is followed by a call to action.
We, as followers and believers of God, must not think we
know everything because we have come to know the truth of
our existence. We need to be malleable and teachable in every
way to become who God has created us to be. Are you
teachable and open to learning new truths? A servant's heart is
a teachable one. Become fearless in being taught by God.

Day 174: Read Proverbs 1:20-33
They had a disdain for knowledge and choose not to fear the Lord.

God wants everyone to seek Him and His knowledge, but those who don't *"will eat the fruit of their ways."* In other words, they've thought more of themselves than God. Their pride has taken over their life, and the consequences will destroy them. When we think we know better than God, we are fooling ourselves. In what area of your life has your pride taken over? Your way is not better than God's. Those who live in His knowledge live without fear of harm. Become fearless in releasing your superiority of pride to God.

Day 175: Read Proverbs 2:1-22
If you keep my words, you will understand the fear of the Lord.

Wisdom, which is a gift from God, is revealed to us through the pages of His Word. When we study the Bible, God enriches our knowledge. Our study is a life-long process, a daily quest for God and His knowledge. Those who seek God will find Him and be rewarded with wisdom! Through the knowledge of the Bible, we understand what it means to fear the Lord and His great power. Do you seek the Lord daily? In what ways are you a wise follower? Grow your wisdom and your knowledge. Become fearless in digging into the Bible daily.

Day 176: Read Proverbs 3:21-35
When you lie down, you will not be afraid or have fear of sudden disaster.

When we trust and believe in God, we have the wisdom, knowledge, and discipline that is rewarded in our confidence of the Lord. Having confidence in the Lord is displayed in us as peace. Are you afraid of sudden disasters or of the evil that overtakes people in the world? We believers sleep peacefully at night, awaken refreshed and do not fear the day to come because our confidence is in the Lord. Relax; He's got this! Become fearless with your faith and confidence in the Lord.

Day 177: Read Proverbs 8:12-36
When you fear the Lord, you must hate all evil.

It's all or nothing when it comes to believing and following God. You can't have one foot in sin and one foot in belief; you cannot pick and choose which sins are tolerable. Tolerating sins of the heart or thoughts is still sin, and tolerating the sins of others is also unacceptable. The more a believer fears and loves God, the less he or she will tolerate any kind of sin. If you fear the Lord, do you hate all evil and sin? God hates sin. Become fearless in the Lord and tolerate no sin from self or others.

Day 178: Read Proverbs 9:10-18
To fear the Lord is the beginning of wisdom and understanding.

Solomon continues to share what he has learned about wisdom from God. In this verse he explains that to be wise is to know God better. To understand God, we need to spend large amounts of time with Him daily. How much of your 24-hour day do you spend with God? Maybe we need to put down the phone and turn off the television for longer periods of time. Learning all about the One with whom we will spend time in eternity makes sense to do now. Become fearless in understanding God better.

Day 179: Read Proverbs 10:27-32
Fearing the Lord adds length to your life.

Not only does fearing the Lord add years to your life, it is a more meaningful life full of righteousness and peace. People usually live longer when they live right and have restful peace in God. They don't fear death because of the free gift of eternal life given by Jesus. These attributes do not come to those who ignore God. Evil ones not only fear death, but miss out on healthy living while here. Do you have peace in your life because of your belief in God? Relax in His truth and become fearless in your gift of eternal life.

Day 180: Read Proverbs 14:1-16
A wise man whose walk is upright fears the Lord, even when fools despise Him.

The upright are full of goodwill and eager to lend a helping hand. They assume the best of others' intentions and help satisfy others' needs before their own. A fool is one who is hotheaded and reckless in life. Fools are often hard to love. How do you show goodwill to others—especially to fools? God's people are full of goodwill and go out of their way to practice being charitable. Become fearless in spreading goodwill for all people.

Day 181: Read Proverbs 14:17-35
Those who fear the Lord have security in this life, and the next.

Those who fear the Lord are secure in His promises. Because of what Jesus did for mankind on the cross, believers know the truth and have security in Him. Those who fear the Lord have the fountain of life! Even in death His beloved believers find refuge. How did God turn you from the snares of death to the fountain of life? As God has shown you, show others the way. Become fearless in your accepted security and share it.

Day 182: Read Proverbs 15:18-33
The fear of the Lord teaches wisdom, humility, and honor.

To fear the Lord is a healthy attitude for the body that teaches true humility. We are reminded of God's greatness and importance in our lives compared to our own importance. We are also reminded in fear of the Lord to remain humble. In God's kingdom, the first will be last and the last will be honored. In what ways are you a humble servant? Remain in awe of God and gain wisdom. Become fearless in seeking humility and the fear of God.

Day 183: Read Proverbs 19:19-29
To fear the Lord leads to a life content and untouched by trouble.

In a perfect world, the fear of the Lord would lead to a life untouched by trouble, but we live in a fallen world full of sin. This general principle will become true in the new world where there is finally no more sin or suffering. Those who fear the Lord become more content and less untouched by trouble, but not exempt. Living wisely by God's laws in our sinful world will lead to a contented life. How do you seek God's wisdom for living your life? The fear of the Lord leads to wisdom and blessings. Rest and rely on God. Become fearless in living a contented life.

Day 184: Read Proverbs 22:1-16
Accept where you are at today
and fear the Lord.

Let's face it, who doesn't want a life of wealth and honor? These kinds of riches cannot be measured by our earthly standards; they are the rewards of being humble. Humility is the process of viewing oneself as less than perfect but perfectly loved by God. We believers are a work-in-progress. We value life right where we're at and cheerfully submit to God. By loving this day and this place, humility has an opportunity to take root. Its benefits are wisdom, peace, long life, wealth, and honor. Are you humble today? Were you humble yesterday? Accept who you are today. God doesn't make mistakes, and He created you to be an individual of wealth and honor. Become fearless in accepting who you are today.

Day 185: Read Proverbs 28:14-28
Blessed is the one who always fears the Lord.

Blessings come in many ways when we fear the Lord. Blessings can be of the heart, mind, and soul. Blessed is the one who will live with God forever in heaven, and God's blessings show today on earth. The person who fears the Lord attains God's favor and protection daily. A blessed one seeks God above all else and lives an upright life of humility and reverence because of that endeavor. What are your blessings today from God? Recognize Him as the supplier of blessings. Become fearless in seeking God's favor.

Day 186: Read Proverbs 31:1-31
The one who fears the Lord is to be praised.

Proverbs 31 describes a woman who fears the Lord. This woman is very capable in many areas, and through her reverence to God, she is courageous and fearless in her household—a role model for sure. Most women cannot live up to her standard of excellence. Therefore, we should look to this proverb for inspiration. When we fear the Lord, we are given admirable qualities because of our reverence for Him. What God-given qualities have you attained? Let hard work, wisdom, compassion, and the fear of God be easily seen in you by living according to God's will. Become fearless in gaining God-given qualities.

ECCLECIASTES

Day 187: Read Ecclesiastes 7:15-22
The one who fears God will avoid living in extremes.

Solomon warns against becoming so rigid in our beliefs that we become inflexible and overly righteous—not needing or fearing God. We believers should fear God and have a healthy reverence for Him. Some extremes to avoid include strict adherence to God's laws without relationship, abstain from immorality, and cease from wickedness. We should follow God's laws but not become dependent on moral law. Rely on your faith and your personal relationship with Jesus. Do you, your friends, or your family live in extremes? Don't even remotely consider these extremes; instead break down the extremes that keep you from God. Become fearless in breaking down personal barriers.

Day 188: Read Ecclesiastes 8:1-17
**Because the wicked do not fear God,
it will not go well with them.**

Solomon reminds us that even if we weren't punished for our wrongs, it doesn't mean God didn't see them, know about them, or care about them. One day we will stand before God and give an answer for our wrongs. The wicked who do not fear God will be punished. While the God-fearing believers are blessed because they are reverent to God, have peace in the unknown, and find joy in each God-given day under the sun. Do you have these blessings under the sun? God's peace and joy are found throughout the Bible. Make every attempt to attain them before the sun goes down. Become fearless in seeking God's blessings.

Day 189: Read Ecclesiastes 12:1-14
**Fear God and keep His commandments;
one day you will stand before Him.**

The conclusion from Solomon in the book of Ecclesiastes is to fear God, then everything else in life falls into place. By making God your first priority, showing Him reverence, and seeking to know Him, life will unfold in the way He planned. Then you will have enjoyment in your work from youth through old age. Continue to obey God and grow in your understanding of Him and your purpose on earth. Do you realize that you will one day stand before God and give a reason for everything that you have done under the sun? Through God we can learn to receive enjoyment in all things. Become fearless in living honestly before God.

ISAIAH

Day 190: Read Isaiah 7:3-9
Keep calm and don't be afraid.

When we have faith in God, we believe in who He is, and trust He will do exactly what He has told us. He knew us before we were born and has set things in motion just for us. Having faith is believing without seeing. The Lord told the prophet Isaiah not to be afraid and not to lose heart because of his circumstances. God also asks the same of us today. In what practice is God asking you to stand firm today? Keep calm and don't be afraid; God will do exactly what He said. Stand firm with faith in God! Become fearless in your current situation.

Day 191: Read Isaiah 8:11-17
Do not fear what they fear.

Getting caught up in what other people are doing and feeling and taking it on as our own beliefs can be easy. But God has asked us to come to Him for our knowledge and rules by which to live. God—not man—shows us how to live. We do not need to fear what the world fears. After all, they do not have God; we do! We are already different and set apart for following Jesus. Do not let fear attack your faith in God. What fears have you falsely taking on as your own? Become fearless in not fearing what others fear.

Day 192: Read Isaiah 10:20-25
Do not be afraid of the Assyrians.

We could easily replace the word *Assyrians* with the names of any of our oppressors. When we seek God in our daily lives, He gives us strength through our faith in Him to become fearless and overcome our oppressors. Who or what is coming after you with a vengeance? Whatever is consuming you has lost its power over you today. Through God's strength, you need not be afraid of them! Become fearless in overcoming oppressors.

Day 193: Read Isaiah 11:1-5
Delight in the fear of the Lord.

Making decisions in life whether big or small are often difficult. We can use our fear of the Lord to guide our actions. When we seek God in our decision-making, we can rest in His assurance of the way to go. Through Him, we are given guidance and strength to carry out our decisions. Remember, our actions have consequences, and one day, we will one day stand before the face of Jesus to give an account. In which decisions did you last seek the help of the Lord? Through His power become fearless in making decisions.

Day 194: Read Isaiah 12:1-6
The Lord is my song, I will trust and not be afraid.

We become fearless when we praise God for everything and through every experience—especially in times of hurt. Even when we mess up, the Lord is always there to comfort us and wants to hear from us. He loves to hear us wholeheartedly praise Him in song. What does your fearless song of praise sound like today? We believers need to fear nothing in this world—only trust and sing God's praises. Become fearless in singing His praise.

Day 195: Read Isaiah 19:16-22
The Egyptians shudder with fear.

Those who have accepted the teachings of Jesus don't need to shudder with fear. We believers know how the story ends. We become fearless in our stake in Jesus Christ! Those who don't know the Lord will have fear now and later. We can become fearless in our approach of others; at any time, they may turn to the Lord, repent, and God will heal them. Who in your life can you see shuddering in fear? Stand strong, and when the Holy Spirit permits, present them with the life-changing gospel of Jesus Christ. Shudder no more! Become fearless to approach those who shudder in fear.

Day 196: Read Isaiah 31:1-9
He is not frightened by their shouts.

The nation of Judah was seeking help from anyone but God. Judah did not want to repent and change their ways to gain the Lord's help; they took matter into their own hands. For Judah to seek help from other nations was wrong. In times of trouble, who did you seek before consulting the Lord? Just ask, God will show you the way to go and send you the necessary help. God is not frightened by anything or anyone, and as believers, our help comes from Him. Become fearless in seeking God first.

Day 197: Read Isaiah 33:1-10
Fear of the Lord is the key to this treasure.

In times of trouble, we find our foundation firm in the salvation of Jesus. Through Him, we gain wisdom and knowledge. In our relationship with Jesus, we store our treasures such as love, joy, peace, patience, kindness, goodness, faithfulness, gentleness, and self-control. Which of these treasures do you have stored? When the world around us comes crashing down, we only fear God. We gain strength and use our key to unlock the treasures we've stored. Become fearless in stored treasures.

Day 198: Read Isaiah 35:1-10
To fearful hearts, be strong and do not fear.

The joy of being redeemed comes in knowing God is ever present to strengthen us. He asks those of us with fearful hearts to be strong and have no fear. He has gone before us and has already made a place for us. This is His encouragement for what is to come. We only need to be strong, keep the faith, and serve Him while we await the final victory. What is your prayer to Jesus as you wait for His return? Believer, be strong! Become fearless in redemption.

Day 199: Read Isaiah 37:1-13
Do not be afraid of what you have heard.

When we come to God with our prayers, we trust He's heard them while we humbly wait for His answer. The task becomes not to let others' words stifle our faith while waiting on God. Sometimes the wait is long, but God has perfect timing. When have you allowed words from a friend, a stranger, or even the news reporting to make you fear? We believers know that our earthly struggles won't last forever, but God will. Become fearless in waiting for answered prayers.

Day 200: Read Isaiah 40:6-14
Lift up your voice with a shout, do not be afraid.

People's opinions about God change like the wind, but God's Word never changes. Even though the world may have a different or even skewed view of who God is, we still have the task to show them the truth. We show them by living it out and shouting it out! Where and when do you give a shout-out for God? When we confidently shout-out who God is and what He has done in our lives, others see a glimpse of Him. The Word of God doesn't change; gain wisdom and confidence from reading the Bible and practice your shout. Become fearless in giving a shout-out to God.

Day 201: Read Isaiah 41:8-20
Do not fear, I am with you.

From generation to generation, God has helped His people. He reminds us that He is with us just as He personally reminded the last generation of believers. He is always with us, will help us, and will uphold us with His righteous right hand! How has God helped you in the past? How is He helping you now? Gain strength by knowing God is with the believers! Become fearless knowing God is with us always.

Day 202: Read Isaiah 43:1-13
Fear not I have called you by name, you are mine.

We are so important to God, the One who has created us and redeemed us. We need not fear because He has summoned us and calls us by our name. When we go it alone and face the trials of this life on our own, our peace will be short-lived. If we turn to our Redeemer for our help and strength, He will protect and guide us always. We are protected because we are His! No one can undo what God has set in motion. How has God been your Protector? He has called us by name, and we are His! Become fearless in His protection.

Day 203: Read Isaiah 44:1-5
Do not be afraid, my chosen one.

Since the very beginning of time, God has chosen us and has provided for us. He delights in giving us the desires of our heart, as well as providing our basic needs. In return, we bear His name with great pride. We believers are unashamed of the gospel of Jesus Christ. Our ancestors wrote on their hands, "*The Lord's,*" for all to see. We become fearless when we proclaim the Lord's name with reckless abandon. How do you show the world that the Lord provides for you? Become fearless as the chosen one.

Day 204: Read Isaiah 50:1-11
Who among you really fears the Lord?

The Israelites forgot about God and didn't fear or include Him in their daily lives. Their sin was having false strength. True strength comes only from God. They forfeited God and continued on in their own power. Human power and strength runs out, but God doesn't. Have you ever accomplished something successfully in your own strength only to realize you couldn't do it again? True strength, accomplishment, and endurance only comes from God. Become fearless in harnessing His true strength.

Day 205: Read Isaiah 51:4-8
Do not fear the reproach of men.

The believers of Jesus Christ will face persecution and even receive insults or criticism from others for our love and belief in Him. We can be encouraged by God whose power and truth is in us, and the truth will set us free from fear. Our persecutors are not against us; they are against God whom we love and represent. When have you been persecuted for your belief in God? Become fearless in knowing the war is against God who has already won!

Day 206: Read Isaiah 51:12-16
Do not fear mortal men for
their days are fleeting.

The overwhelming power of Babylon instilled fear into the people of Jerusalem who feared them more than God. Jerusalem feared that the armies of Babylon would terrorize and hold them captive. They forgot the power of God is much greater than that of man, and He only wants to set us free from fear. What in this life has taken you captive? Remember that we, the believers of Jesus Christ, have been set free, and the power of God lives in us! Become fearless knowing God's power is greater than all.

Day 207: Read Isaiah 54:1-8
Do not be afraid, and do not fear disgrace.

God reminds us that we will not be humiliated or fear the disgrace of our youth. The life we led before we met Jesus is gone and over. At salvation, we became new creations in Him. In accepting His truth, we no longer live in sin. We are prone to sin, but we know better and try to do be different. Our shame and disgrace is wiped clean by His compassion. We are called to live fearless lives, free of guilt and shame. What are the differences between your old self of your youth and you today? Praise God for calling you out of sin and bringing you back home. Become fearless knowing you are made right with God.

Day 208: Read Isaiah 57:1-21
God asked the wicked who they feared more than Him.

The Jewish people had begun worshiping false gods, and the only true God wanted to know why. God asked the most thought-provoking question of all: "Whom do you fear that you have been false to Me?" He wanted to know who was so much greater and who would demand the fear that He rightfully acquired. Those who have no care or concern for God show no fear of Him. Who has taken the place of God in your heart, causing you to harbor fear? The only fear a believer should entertain is a healthy fear of awe, wonder, respect, and love reserved entirely for God. Don't let your fears crowd out God. He is the only One to be feared! Become fearless in your reverence for God.

Day 209: Read Isaiah 59:1-21
All will come to fear the name of the Lord.

The bottom line is that God hates sin, and our unconfessed sin separates us from God. With our acceptance of Jesus and the realization of salvation, we believers are now free from our sinful nature. Through redemption and the Holy Spirit, people gain a changed heart which pleases God. What has changed the most about you since you started following Jesus? Grow into the person He created you to be. Confess, rid yourself of sin, and be filled with the change that's pleasing to God. Become fearless in changing your ways to God's ways.

JEREMIAH

Day 210: Read Jeremiah 1: 1-19
The Lord is with you, do not be afraid.

The Lord is the One who puts His words into our mouths. He is the One who gives us the words to speak and share with others. God gives us strength to carry out any mission or work He assigns. We need to step forward in faith and complete the tasks He has given. What is He asking of you today? He knew you before you were born and created a work for you to complete. Use His words for you! Become fearless in completing the work.

Day 211: Read Jeremiah 5:1-31
They did not fear God nor tremble before Him.

God searched the city of Jerusalem to find just one person who respected Him, but sadly, He found none because the people didn't fear Him. We should heed the error of their arrogance and pay our due respects to God today. Our God is one of awe and wonder. He tells the waves where to stop and the land where to begin. He has placed a boundary in the sand, and the waves obey it. He has also placed a boundary around our hearts and asks us to obey His Word. How do pay respects to God both privately and publically? When we respect and honor God, we become fearless through Him, and others can see His greatness. Become fearless in respecting God in all ways.

Day 212: Read Jeremiah 8:4-22
The whole land will tremble in fear
of their punishment.

The people of Jerusalem have rejected the Word of God, sinned against Him, and ignored their behavior. They have lived as if the way they were living would have no consequences. Our God-given instinct when we fall down is to get back up, dust ourselves off, and change direction. Jerusalem didn't change direction or repent; they continued on in their sin. Even the birds of the air obey their God-given instinct for migration, but God's people often do not. We believers know that when we sin, we are convicted of that behavior by the Holy Spirit, and we should come before God with a repentant heart in prayer asking for His forgiveness. In what area of your life have you overlooked and become like the residents of Jerusalem in Jeremiah's day? God is waiting to hear from you. Become fearless in obeying your God-given instincts of repentance.

Day 213: Read Jeremiah 10:1-16
Do not tremble in fear by the signs of the sky
or the nations that fear them.

The people of the world are looking for signs and have erroneously placed their trust in many different idols. Some worship the stars in the sky, others an ornately carved block of wood; all are substitutes for God. Idols and false beliefs have made their way into our everyday life. We believers place our trust in the only One who has created the stars and the wood that others are foolishly worshiping. Do you fear what others fear about the future? Place your trust in God alone who holds it. Become fearless in trusting God with your future.

Day 214: Read Jeremiah 14:1-22
We hoped for peace but there is only fear
because of wickedness and guilt.

Jeremiah petitioned God on behalf of the people, but God didn't want to hear his prayers. The hearts of Jerusalem's people were sinful and insincere in seeking God. The people knew they should repent of their sins, so they did, but they didn't stop sinning. True repentance equals a changed life. In what area of your life do you need God's forgiveness and direction to make a needed change? Be willing to stop doing what is wrong today. Become fearless in change.

Day 215: Read Jeremiah 17:1-18
He will live as a tree planted near the water
that does not fear when the heat comes.

In this verse, the prophet Jeremiah is talking about two kinds of people: those who trust in man and those who put their trust in God. The nation of Judah's sin angered God because they had placed their trust in the strength of their own men and were also worshiping false gods. Those who put their trust in the Lord were blessed and had no fears—even in times of trouble. Where is your trust placed? Do you rely on the strength of people around you, or are you a well-watered tree leaning on God? Even well-watered trees need to remember to lean on God in times of trouble. Trust in God's strength. Become fearless in depending on God in all times.

Day 216: Read Jeremiah 22:18-30
God's judgment was coming for Jehoiakim who will be handed over to his fears.

A signet ring is a notable and prized possession worn by a person in authority to validate documents. God told Jehoiakim even if he were His signet ring, He would pull it off and hand it over to his worst fears. This king was useless to God because his desire for prosperity and success far outweighed his desire for God. He simply didn't have time for Him. Therefore, God did not find Jehoikim to be a useful vessel because of his sinful nature. When you are pressed for time during the week is God on your list of priorities? Ask yourself what is more important, then do that. Don't be so busy trying to make a life that you forget to build a relationship with God. All God's believers are His prized possessions; make Him yours. Stay useful to Him and remain with the hand of God. Become fearless in making God the priority.

Day 217: Read Jeremiah 23:1-8
God will place shepherds over them, and they will no longer be afraid.

God harshly judged the kings of Judah and warned others like them. Even today, our church leaders are held responsible and will be judged more harshly than others because they have been appointed by God to deliver His message and shepherd His people. Every leader needs to be led by God and is held accountable for influencing lives. Who has God placed in your care? Who is leading you? Gain strength from God, lead those whom He has entrusted to your care, and don't leave anyone behind. Become a fearless shepherd.

Day 218: Read Jeremiah 26:1-19
**Hezekiah feared the Lord,
and so did Jeremiah.**

God told Jeremiah to deliver His message to the people and not to omit a word. He obeyed God and boldly proclaimed His message. Though the people became enraged, Jeremiah did not back down. He did not fear the people—only God. The people spared Jeremiah's life when they remembered the great faith of King Hezekiah, his fear of the Lord and how the Lord had fought His battles. Have you ever given an indirect answer about God to avoid a conflict and keep the peace? God wants us to be peacemakers, but not at the cost of the kingdom. Give people the whole story; don't dilute God's Word. Be bold and speak for the Lord. Become fearless in speaking God's truth.

Day 219: Read Jeremiah 26:20-24
The prophet Uriah fled in fear of the king.

Uriah, the man of God, faithfully spoke God's Word like the prophet Jeremiah. He prophesied the same messages against the city, but his story had the opposite outcome. When Uriah's prophesies reached the palace, evil King Jehoiakim planned to put him to death. Uriah fled in fear, was captured, and struck down with a sword. Do you think Uriah would have had a different outcome if He had stayed and stood his ground? God calls for His people to be bold and courageous for Him, and He gives us His strength to do it. Become fearless in seeking the boldness of God.

Day 220: Read Jeremiah 30:1-24
Do not fear, the Lord will save you.

God heard the cries of His people, and through Jeremiah's words, He promised to restore them with a new covenant. This promise was the hope of turning a sinful nation into one of true repentance and obedience. God's promise of restoration for Judah and Israel is still offered to every believer today. God still promises us a rescue of a lifetime, if we will accept Jesus as our Lord and Savior, submit, repent, obey, and accept His unconditional love. Have you accepted the Son of God as your Savior? If you have, then from today forward, you need have no fear! God has taken it from you and given you a promise of salvation. Become fearless in His promise.

Day 221: Read Jeremiah 32:1-44
I will give them a heart of oneness so they will always fear me for their own good.

Jeremiah trusted God enough to buy enemy territory though it wasn't easy. Trusting God is a two-part process. Step one is making the decision to trust, and step two is following through. Trust what God asks you to do for Him, and He will bless your actions and your following through for His kingdom. Trusting is a front row seat to watch God work in our lives. What profound change do you need in your life to trust God in the biblical way? When Jeremiah doubted God, he prayed and repeated every truth He knew about Him. Become fearless in flawlessly trusting God.

Day 222: Read Jeremiah 36:1-32
The king heard the word of God,
yet had no fear or respect.

When King Jehoiakim heard the words of God written on the scroll, he had no fear and burned them. Even though the king burned the scroll, he couldn't extinguish the Word of God; nobody can. God's Word is written on our hearts, minds, and souls. Many may claim to believe yet have no fear of God or His Word. How well do you know and respect the Word of God? True believers will study, stand out, and stand up for God's Word. This is not a verbal battle; this one is simply displayed in respect, honor, and right living with God. Become fearless in learning God's Word.

Day 223: Read Jeremiah 38:1-28
King Zedekiah was afraid of the Jews
and afraid to trust God's message.

Zedekiah trusted Jeremiah as a faithful prophet—enough to rescue him and swear a secret oath to spare his life from whatever he had prophesied. King Zedekiah trusted God's messenger, but he was still apprehensive to follow God's advice. As God's messengers, we can only do what God has asked and given us authority to carry out. By following through, our task is complete. What others do with the message is between them and God. When sharing God's message, have you ever felt the obligation to make others take the advice from God and follow through? God frees us from that obligation and reminds us that's His job. Do your part. Deliver the message, and then let go. Become fearless in faithfully proclaiming God's message.

Day 224: Read Jeremiah 39:1-18
The Lord will rescue you and spare you from those you fear.

The Lord warned King Zedekiah through His messenger, Jeremiah, that his kingdom would be overtaken by Babylon. However, Zedekiah failed to heed God's warnings. When Babylon came, God rescued Jeremiah because of his great faith, and the opposite was true for Zedekiah who was killed because of his fear. Another one of God's faithful men, Ebed-Melech the Cushite, was also rescued by God and not handed over to the ones he feared. God's pattern is to protect and provide for His faithful. Are you faithful to God—no matter your circumstances? When we give up our catastrophic fear, we become faithful to God—no matter what comes our way. God rewards those who are faithful. Whether we receive our reward in this life or in the next one will be the surprise. Become fearless in being faithful to God.

Day 225: Read Jeremiah 40:1-16
Do not be afraid to settle down and serve them, and it will go well with you.

The Babylonian commander, Nebuzaradan, knew who God was and what He had done for him, but still did not accept Him. He appointed Gedaliah to reassure God's faithful to have no fear and serve the Babylonians in cultivating the land for them and sharing in the harvest. The people received the solemn oath of a man named Gedaliah, as well as a promise from God to provide for His faithful. How has God provided for you through another? God is the ultimate Provider, and He can turn our worries into trust through His provisions. Become fearless in His provisions.

Day 226: Read Jeremiah 42:1-22
Do not be afraid; God is with you
and will save you.

The people sought God's guidance through Jeremiah, the prophet. They did not like what he had to say and thought he was lying. The people went their own way—even with warnings from God and entered Egypt. Have you ever sought God's guidance with no intention of following it? You knew in your heart what was right to do, but you willfully chose not to do it. When we disrespect God and go against His guidance, we will surely fail. Do not be afraid; God hears your prayers. Become fearless in following through in prayer requests.

Day 227: Read Jeremiah 46:25-28
Do not fear or be afraid; I am with you.

God punished His people to get their attention and to get them to return to Him. He didn't want them to continue to seek other gods and worship them. God is a jealous God, who asked us in the Ten Commandments to have no other God but Him. When we do wrong, God disciplines us to get us to return to Him. Even though He corrects us, He never leaves us. How has God got your attention and disciplined you in the past or even now? God disciplines with justice and purity of heart. Become fearless in accepting God's correction.

Day 228: Read Jeremiah 51:1-32
In battle the soldiers were terrified.

The soldiers of Babylon had finished serving God's purpose of punishing the people of Judah for their sins. The people of Babylon were as wicked and sinful as those they were being used to punish. Since God was no longer fighting their battles, the soldiers were terrified. The Lord was now with the kings of the Medes and had directed them to conquer Babylon. Ever try fighting your own battles in your power? What a daunting task! We run out of stamina, strength, and tire easily, but when the Lord is fighting our battles, we cannot lose. Don't go it alone! Invite God to fight for you and listen to His directions. Become fearless in fighting with the Lord's guidance.

Day 229: Read Jeremiah 51:33-64
God told the Jews not to lose heart
or be afraid of the rumors.

God warned the Jews to flee from Babylon before the upcoming battle. Following God's message meant they would be spared from the sword. God also told them not lose heart or be afraid of the rumors. He warned all of the Jews in Babylon to leave before the battle ensued. When God warned you about a certain matter, did you listen to Him? When we hear rumors of the world's coming to an end or we're living in end times because nation is warring against nation, recognize God has spared us and given us eternal life. We believers don't need to fear what the rest of the world fears. Even though everything was crumbling around the Jews, God's faithful remnant didn't lose heart. Don't lose heart and adhere to God's warnings. Become fearless in hearing rumors.

LAMENTATIONS

Day 230: Read Lamentations 3:1-66
You heard my call, came near,
and told me to have no fear.

God provided for Jeremiah in his darkest times, and as he reflected on those dark days, God reminded His weeping prophet of the hope He offered to those who were obedient to Him. As Jeremiah wept over the people consumed by sin, he was reminded that God is the faithful provider of love and compassion. Recognizing that the people were being punished for their sins, but he remained hopeful they would repent and change. Only then would God forgive and show them love. For whom do you pray on a regular basis to know God? Continually call out the names of unsaved people to God, and petition Him on their behalf. Become fearless in never-ceasing prayers for the unsaved.

EZEKIEL

Day 231: Read Ezekiel 1:1-28 and 2:1-8
Do not be afraid of a rebellious nation.

The prophet Ezekiel chose to obey God's very specific call on his life. The vision God sent must have been overwhelming for him to witness and understand. God asked Ezekiel to serve Him by relaying His message to a rebellious nation and not to be afraid of them or their words. Even though we don't understand everything about God, we can serve as His messengers. God did not judge Ezekiel on how well his message was received; He only judged him by his willingness to obey His request. How well do you obey God when He calls you to serve? God's will is done on earth through His imperfect servants. Become fearless in obedience to God's call.

Day 232: Read Ezekiel 3:1-27
Do not be afraid of them; I will
make you stronger.

When God calls us, He has already made a way for us and is always ten steps or more ahead of us. When God told Ezekiel to eat the scroll and then go and speak those words to the rebellious people, He was strengthening His prophet for the task. Ezekiel was the one God chose to warn Israel. When God calls us into action, He prepares us and gives us everything needed to complete the mission. Just as we take care of our physical bodies, we also need to take care of our spiritual bodies. We do this spending time in prayer and reading the Word of God. How well are you caring for your spiritual body? Make time for God daily and let Him prepare you for running your race for His glory. Become fearless in God's conditioning.

Day 233: Read Ezekiel 11:1-25
Fear the sword; you have not kept my laws
and conformed to those around you.

Ezekiel fearlessly delivered God's message to the Israelites. The twenty-five men at the gate represented Israel's leaders who were responsible for leading the people astray. The leaders gave the people a false security, letting them believe they were safe from the Babylonians. God declared that since the people did not keep His laws and had conformed to the standards of the world around them, they would fear the sword that would be brought against them. How well do you keep from conforming to the world around you? As believers, we already stand out from the crowd in thought, action, and belief. Keep it that way! Don't allow any part of your life to conform to the norms of this world. Focus on the next! Become fearless in not conforming to the ways of the world.

133

Day 234: Read Ezekiel 12:1-28
The rebellious people will shudder in fear as they live their lives unchanged by God.

When Ezekiel warned the rebellious people of God's words, many refused to hear him. They continued to live their lives as if God's warnings were untrue and would never happen. The people believed in false prophets and visionaries instead of God whose dire warnings came true. God's warnings will one day come true for us. Do you think you have plenty of time to get right with God? Christ will return at a time only known by God. Get ready! Become fearless in adhering to the warnings from God.

Day 235: Read Ezekiel 26:1-21
Tyre's neighbors were terrified at its collapse.

Tyre was well-known around the world as a place of commerce and trade. Supplies were easily imported and exported from all sides of the Tyre peninsula which projected into the Mediterranean Sea. The city was heavily fortified, making it a difficult place to conquer. The people became so prideful and powerful as a nation that their neighbors feared them. Ezekiel delivered God's prophecy against Tyre. The sovereign Lord declared that all of Tyre's neighbors would be completely clothed in terror and sit trembling at its collapse. The princes trembled in fear of what would happen to them next. Is there anything in your life that you've given as much power as Tyre was given? God can bring down any mighty and powerful city like Tyre. No one can stand against God. Reserve your power, only handing it over to God. Become fearless in recognizing God as being the all-powerful One.

Day 236: Read Ezekiel 27:1-36
All who saw Tyre shuddered with fear
of their bitter end.

Ezekiel warned the people of Tyre that the end was near for them. Their pride guaranteed their harsh judgment from God. When we control our own lives without concern for how or when God fits in, we too, will be judged like Tyre. The people of Tyre tried to get by on their own merits, and God was not included. We believers know that we only get by with God's guidance. He is the source of our existence. Have you ever experienced success without God being involved? Ungodly success will be short-lived; go all out and include Him in every area of your life. Become fearless in attaining success through God's guidance.

Day 237: Read Ezekiel 30:1-26
The day is near and fear spread
throughout the land.

Because the Nile River was their source of life, the Egyptians claimed that they had made the river. God told the Egyptian people that He would dry up the river and sell off their land to evil men to show them who had made the river and everything else. This decree was a clear message to Egypt and its allies that God is the only One to be trusted and feared. Because of their arrogance, God spread fear throughout the land. We believers do not have to live in fear of God's wrath. We have accepted and placed our trust in Him. Have you ever thought yourself to be superior on a subject matter and couldn't hear anyone else? Remember who our Superior is and listen to Him. Become fearless in His superiority.

Day 238: Read Ezekiel 31:1-18
The nations will tremble at the sound
of Lebanon's fall.

Ezekiel prophesied many judgments from God on the fall of many evil nations. God proved that justice comes to evil nations and people like the felling of a tree. Ezekiel delivered God's message of judgment to Pharaoh, the king of Egypt, using the comparison of a magnificent cedar tree, meaning Egypt would soon fall like the powerful Assyrians. The Lord would cut down Egypt because of their pride and strength and put the nation in its place. What evil in your life do you need God to cut down and root out? God has shown He does not tolerate our pride or when we do things in our own strength. Take your eyes off yourself and put them back on Jesus. Become fearless in releasing your pride.

Day 239: Read Ezekiel 32:1-32
All who spread terror will be punished.

The Egyptians were concerned with the afterlife but not with God. They thought they could control both their present and future lives. Ezekiel's words that came directly from God revealed the Egyptians' coming judgment. They would soon experience the very terror they had inflicted on others. When has the life of another caused you hurt? In this life, we will have those who hate us and oppose us because we are the believers of Jesus Christ. Remember, your God is mighty, and He has the last say. Become fearless in those opposing you.

Day 240: Read Ezekiel 34:1-31
No one will make us afraid; God has provided every need.

Ezekiel criticized the leaders of Israel and compared them to shepherds not properly herding their sheep, saying they were not concerned about their sheep—only with their own well-being. God will hold them accountable for their selfish misuse of leadership. God Himself pledged to be the Shepherd to bring back His flock to safety from the scattered places. How has God asked you to lead others? How did you do? As our great Leader and Provider, God operates through our selfless obedience to Him. Go where He is leading. Shepherd the areas He's asked you to. Become fearless in following His lead.

Day 241: Read Ezekiel 39:1-29
God will forget the shame of Israel, and no one will make them afraid.

Ezekiel delivered God's prophecy against Gog, proclaiming that no longer would His holy name be profaned. The final defeat was coming for God's enemies, and He was about to restore the land. Through the destruction, Israel and the surrounding nations would realize that God is to be feared. Then God will gather and show compassion on Israel who will no longer be afraid. The Lord's name would be known and feared by all nations. Any enemy of God is our enemy as well, and we don't face our enemies on our own. The fearless One goes before us and calls us to be the same. What enemy territory are you walking through with God? Remember there is no one to make you afraid. Remain faithful to Him and let Him fight your battles. Become fearless in the face of your enemies.

DANIEL

Day 242: Read Daniel 5:1-31
Do not be alarmed, there is a man who has the
Spirit of God in him.

Daniel was not motivated by rewards; he did God's work to bring glory to His kingdom. Using the gifts God gave him, Daniel desired to please the King. He also delighted in striving to do what was right, thereby pleasing the Lord. God gave Daniel the ability to interpret the mysterious three-word message written on the wall. Even when the message was a hard one to deliver, Daniel had no fear. He honored God and delivered the fateful message. How do you honor God? Do you do what is right? Be motivated by His love and the eternal rewards that will come one day. Keep the Spirit of God in you! Become fearless in doing what is right without any reward.

Day 243: Read again, Daniel 5:1-31
The king was frightened; his face turned pale,
and his knees knocked together.

King Belshazzar was fearful that no one in his kingdom could decipher the message written on the wall by a ghostly hand. Then the queen remembered a man who had the gift of the Holy Spirit and would be able to decipher the message. The man's name was Daniel, and he was known to be able to interpret dreams. Daniel told the king to keep his gifts and revealed his days were numbered, and he would fall because of his pride, idol worship, and misuse of power. The king was unfaithful to God. When we aren't following God's way, things in this world can be used to terrify us like King Belshazzar was terrified. What fears have you let go of since being in God's way? God's faithful attain His power and peace, which enables them to let go of fears. We no longer fear what the world fears. Become fearless in letting go of every last fear.

Day 244: Read Daniel 6:1-28
Daniel had no fear; God's angel shut
the mouths of the lions.

Daniel already knew the consequences of his actions, but he had no fear and continued praying. He didn't fear man or man's actions; he feared God alone. Daniel prayed openly to God with a peaceful heart, fully trusting Him. When King Darius saw the servant of the living God had been supernaturally protected, he issued a new decree that everyone must fear and worship Daniel's God. Daniel's obedient testimony impacted an entire nation of peoples. How has God given you peace and rescued you in times of great trouble? Let God use your testimony to impact others. Become fearless in trusting God with your life.

Day 245: Read Daniel 7:1-28
Daniel was terrified of the beast with iron teeth
that crushed and devoured.

Daniel saw this vision when Belshazzar had just become king. The apostle John also had a similar vision he recorded in the book of Revelation. In this vision, Daniel saw four kingdoms portrayed as a lion, a bear, a leopard, and a beast that would rise from the earth. The beast representing one of the kingdoms was terrifyingly different from the others. With its ten horns, the beast would devour the entire earth, trampling and crushing it—but only for a time. As war in the kingdom raged on, a new ruler would appear, and His kingdom would be an everlasting one. At that time, the beast would be destroyed once and for all. God allowed Daniel and John to see these visions. What vision has God allowed you to see? Daniel was pale and terrified from the vision, but he had the promise that God's faithful would prevail. The war was already won! Become fearless as the end times approach.

139

Day 246: Read Daniel 8:1-27
As the angel Gabriel came near, Daniel was terrified and fell face down.

Daniel had another vision during the third year of Belshazzar's reign as king. This time the Lord sent His heavenly messenger, the angel Gabriel, to interpret his dream. As the angel came near, Daniel fell face down, completely terrified. The angel warned the prophet about a wicked master of intrigue who would arise and succeed in bringing devastation and destruction to the holy people. Later, the wicked master would be destroyed forever. Just like God allowed Daniel to see this vision of the distant future, He allows us to see our own warnings from Him. How has God warned you? Even though these warnings may not come often, obey these warnings. Become fearless in whatever God permits you to see.

Day 247: Read Daniel 10:1-21
Do not be afraid, child of God; be strong now!

Daniel fervently prayed to God for three weeks, asking Him to reveal the message in the vision. The vision was the battle of good versus evil. God sent a messenger to Daniel, and his arrival frightened him so much he fell trembling, losing his speech and strength. God's messenger touched Daniel and restored his speech. The messenger spoke words of truth and instructed him to be strong. These words gave the prophet strength. How has God strengthened you through fervent prayer? Keep praying, never giving up. He will provide answers in His perfect timing. Expect God to answer your prayers. Become fearless in fervent prayer.

HOSEA

Day 248: Read Hosea 11:1-11
He will roar like a lion and His children will come trembling and repent.

God the Lion will roar and display terrible signs of His anger, and His children will fear and quickly obey Him. Those who do not believe will hear the roar as sounds of terror, but to those who believe, it is the strength and roar of God's reminding His people to come home. The roar—the powerful voice of the gospel—is calling out to God's people today as in the past. The roar is the call to repent. Have you accepted the loud and powerful roar of the gospel of God? Now is the time to repent! Become fearless in obeying His roar.

Day 249: Read Hosea 13:1-16
The Lord will give them over to their enemies to be torn apart like a lion.

The Lord possessed a fierce anger against Israel because His people had rebelled and forgotten Him. When life gets busy, we can forget about God if we're not careful and mindful of Him. When life is good, we tend not to need God and even fail to include Him in our life. Commit yourself to God and subdue His wrath. Remember that every gift and blessing is from God. Are you committed in your relationship with God? Don't become like Israel and forget Him; confirm your commitment to Him. Become fearless in your commitment to God.

AMOS

Day 250: Read Amos 3:1-10
The roar of the Lord is loud.
Do you fear Him?

We cannot claim to love God, hear His voice, and not obey Him. God, the mighty Lion of Judah, has roared and warned of the judgment to come. The people then and the people now must address their sin before it's too late. The longer we ignore our sins and keep on sinning, the more we forget about God. What sin in your life are you ignoring? The lion has roared; choose to fear Him. Become fearless in obeying God.

JONAH

Day 251: Read Jonah 1:1-10
In fear Jonah ran away from the Lord.

Jonah knew that God had a specific job for him to do, and instead of obeying, the prophet ran and hid from God's calling. When God gives us a task, it often seems too big for us, and we're right. The task is too big for us in our humanness, but not for God. When we are faithful to God and follow Him, He gives us His power and strength to complete any work He delegates to us. What has God asked you to do that you're running from and avoiding? Stop running! He knows right where you are and will meet you there. Become fearless in completing God-given tasks.

Day 252: Read Jonah 1:11-17
As the seas calmed, the men greatly feared the Lord and made vows to Him.

When Jonah saw the great storm was a direct result of his disobedience to God, he quickly admitted his fault and repented. The consequence for his disobedience was being thrown overboard. The seas calmed immediately, and the men on the ship watched God's miracle. God used Jonah's mistake and disobedience to bring unbelievers to repentance. God wants all people to be saved and know Him. How has God turned your mistakes and disobedience into good for the kingdom? Become fearless in admitting your mistakes before God.

MICAH

Day 253: Read Micah 6:1-16
The Lord is warning the city; fearing His name is wise.

God wants to be part of our daily life—not just when we warm a seat in a pew on a Sunday. He expects changed hearts and lives because we know and believe in Him. We become wise as we walk with God. Israel was trying to please God with unlimited sacrifices, but the people were far from Him. They were merely going through the motions. God wants us to be living sacrifices and for our actions to be an extension of who He is. How do you act justly, love mercifully, and walk humbly with God? God has shown us in His Word what is good, wise, and how to walk humbly with Him. Become fearless in becoming a living sacrifice to God.

143

Day 254: Read Micah 7:8-20
They will come trembling from everywhere in the fear of God.

God, who is the epitome of forgiveness, waits patiently for us to return to Him and repent. Those who are steadfast believers and followers need to prepare to help make a way for God to reach the others. Become a beacon of light for all of God's creation. When anyone seeks your help because of trusting in your relationship and knowledge of God, come alongside of them and share your knowledge of spiritual matters. When God's people come out of every corner of the earth to know Him better, welcome them with open arms. Are you ready for those who are afraid of you and your God? When you walk humbly with God, others will notice and want what you have. Become fearless in sharing who God is with others.

NAHUM

Day 255: Read Nahum 1:1-15
The whole world trembles at His presence.

The Lord is good and cares for those who trust Him. Those who do not have complete allegiance to God will be punished. God is slow to anger, but when He does get ready to punish evil, the whole earth will tremble in fear. God punishes His children to remove sin from our lives and restore peace. God's will is that none should perish, but He won't wait patiently forever. Though He continues to give His followers time to evangelize the unbelievers and evildoers in this world, judgment day will come. How do you show love through God's Word to the everyday skeptics? He's counting on you and holding the clock for their benefit. Become fearless in spreading His Word until the time is up.

Day 256: Read Nahum 2:1-13
She is pillaged and trembles while the lions
have nothing to fear.

The Assyrian people have been referred as lions prowling, devouring, and taking anything they wanted with nothing to fear. They robbed the innocent in order to continue living their lavish lifestyles. The Assyrians living in Nineveh were given the opportunity to repent, but they chose not to believe, passing the point of no return. We believers have a moral obligation given by God to stand up for injustice. We will be judged for ignoring such sin. If we all did our part, the world would be a far better place. If you will do your part, others will see you, and join in! Where do you give your time, talents, and money to make a difference in local, national, or global injustices in the world? Become fearless in standing up for injustice in God's world.

HABAKKUK
Day 257: Read Habakkuk 1:1-17
A nation is rising up that will be feared and dreaded.

Habakkuk poured out his heart to the Lord and questioned what many of us still wonder today: *Why does God allow evil and evil people to go unpunished?* The Lord answered Habakkuk's first complaint. He would amaze his prophet with a powerful nation that will rise up. This new nation will be feared and dreaded by all. God was handling the corruption and sin Habakkuk was seeing with a plan of His own. God is a lifetime of steps ahead of us; we cannot fathom all that He has planned. God is in control, He has a plan, and He will punish when He's ready. What amazing and powerful sights has God allowed you to see thus far? Don't doubt God; let Him amaze and show you that you are a powerful nation just like the one He was describing. God's plan is always better than yours! Become fearless while you wait for victory.

Day 258: Read Habakkuk 2:1-20
The time will come when evil will tremble.

In Habakkuk's second complaint to God, he still questioned why God would use evil to punish evil. The Lord answered His prophet by instructing him to be patient, to wait, and see. Everything is in God's timing and plan; we need to be patient like He asked. The matter of patience all boils down to trusting. How well do you trust God and believe He is who He says He is? When we trust God with *some things* but not *everything*, then *nothing* is at peace. It isn't easy to be patient. Merely waiting behind two people to check out seems endless. At the same time, don't mistake patience for the inability to move. Do your part around you. God works through His believers. Work while you wait! Become fearless in trusting God to work in His timing.

Day 259: Read Habakkuk 3:1-10
God shook the earth and made the
nations tremble.

Habakkuk praised God for His awesome majesty and for answering his questions. He accepted the fact that those he knew would experience grave discipline, and he might not even be exempt from God's wrath. Sometimes we can do nothing about others having to learn hard lessons, except to pray to God. And sometimes we learn those hard lessons right alongside of them. God disciplines the ones He loves to bring them back to Him. What harsh lesson did you learn from God? Many great life lessons are learned from God's loving discipline. Learn from Him. Become fearless in learning in times of discipline.

Day 260: Read Habakkuk 3:11-19
His legs trembled, but he waited
patiently on the Lord.

Habakkuk's legs trembled because of the affliction he knew his people would soon endure. He knew troubled times were coming his way, but he chose to praise God and patiently wait on His timing. He praised God for being the source of his strength. We can't successfully do life on our own or in our own power. We can't fight evil with human strength. We can only fight evil with supernatural power—the strength of God. When we operate in our own strength, we experience doubt and fear. Essentially, we are saying to God that we don't need Him or His power. We receive His strength when we believe in Him by putting our trust in Him, surrendering our weaknesses, and gaining His strength. When was the last time you received God's strength? When you find your legs trembling and see trouble come your way, stand strong, using the power from God. Become fearless in His strength.

ZEPHANIAH

Day 261: Read Zephaniah 3:1-7
Will you accept my correction and fear me?

The people of Jerusalem pretended to know God, but their hearts were far from Him. Their hearts had become hardened, and no matter what God did, they did not seek Him nor listen to Him. The people continued to sin and lost their desire to know God. The people were so prideful that they could not hear or simply ignored God's conviction or discipline. How does your pride get in the way as it did with the Israelites living in Jerusalem? God corrects His people because He loves them and wants them to have an abundantly full life. Become fearless in obeying God's correction.

147

Day 262: Read again, Zephaniah 3:1-7
The Lord told the city of Jerusalem
that they will fear Him!

Zephaniah spoke truth about God's coming wrath and destruction on Jerusalem, but the people would not comply with the correction of the Lord. The people went through the outward motions of serving God, but their hearts were far from Him; they continued in their sin. Even though Jerusalem was full of unbelieving sinners, God was still in the city. Looking around, we may feel like we're living in a wayward Jerusalem, but remember God is with us. Is God doing something in your community in which you could be involved? Zephaniah delivered God's message with the kind of strength and boldness that only God can give. Let God use you where He is working in your community. Show the people how to fear God again. Just show up; He'll tell you what to do. Become fearless in working with God right where you are.

Day 263: Read Zephaniah 3:8-20
The meek and the humble will rest and
no one will make them afraid.

God restores hope and patience by reminding the people that judgment day will come. For those who have been obedient to the Lord, it will be a glorious day. God describes how the lips of all people will be purified. On judgment day, the condemnation of the Tower of Babel will be reversed; in heaven all will speak the same language. Can you imagine being able to speak to all of God's children and hear their stories? No wonder heaven is called eternity. We will need eons of time to hear and tell our endless stories. No one will be left who will cause fear. No fear today because of a glorious tomorrow. Become fearless in hope.

HAGGAI

Day 264: Read Haggai 1:1-15
And all the people feared the Lord and pursued Him first.

The people did not think the time had come to rebuild the temple, but the Lord had delivered a message through His servant Haggai. The Lord would be pleased to be honored in the temple. Oftentimes we think we know what God wants, but we must slow down and inquire of the Lord. The people feared God when they realized He was their first priority. Do you seek God's guidance in every situation—good or bad? Or do you only seek Him in times of trouble or failure? Seek Him before your first step in any direction. Become fearless in seeking Him first.

Day 265: Read Haggai 2:1-9
Do not fear, God's spirit is always with you.

In God's second message through the prophet Haggai, He instructed the people to be strong, to do the work set before them, and to fear not; God was and would always be with them. God has given each of us a specific work to do. We must complete the work in every area of our life or His will won't be done. Where in your life are you failing to do His work? Oftentimes, we are good at regularly reading and studying our Bibles, but we seemingly forget to be His hands and feet in the community. God is always with you! Become fearless in completing the work He's given you to do.

ZECHARIAH

Day 266: Read Zechariah 8:1-23
Do not be afraid; the Lord has given you complete instructions.

The Lord asks us to speak truth to each other in love and to live peaceably with another. In return, God will faithfully bless those who follow through on His instructions. God is pleased when we live peacefully with others and speak the truth in love. He is displeased when we plot evil against others and give a false testimony. If we expect God to do His part, we must do ours. What can you do today to live peaceably with others? Do not be afraid to be the one who initiates change. Become fearless in following God's complete instructions.

MALACHI

Day 267: Read Malachi 3:1-18 and 4:1-6
The Lord will judge those who do not fear Him.

The Lord's judgment will come against those who do not fear Him and have done wrong in His eyes. When we do God's will for our life, our willingness to live for him will become apparent to those who do not know Him, as well as to those believers who live their lives without the fear of God. The faithful who fear God will be honored by His name, become His treasured possession, and will be spared. Are you God's treasured possession? Is He yours? The Lord calls His believers by name; we are His! Become fearless in remaining His.

MATTHEW

Day 268: Read Matthew 1:18-23
Joseph, do not be afraid to take
Mary as your wife.

God sends His angels to protect His children, to deliver messages, and to offer guidance. In this passage, God sent an angel to guide Joseph in his decision to accept Mary as his wife. After learning Mary was with child, Joseph could only see two options; however, God sent His reinforcement for a third. When faced with difficult decisions that affect others, we often only see the surface. God sees what's underneath. When making decisions, do you seek God first or only when you are in trouble? In difficult decisions, always consider God first; His may be the option you never considered. When we allow God to guide our lives, His will is done. Become fearless in seeking God in times of indecision.

Day 269: Read Matthew 2:1-23
Joseph was afraid to go, so he heeded God's
warning and moved to Nazareth.

After Herod's death, his three sons occupied his position of power. One son assumed power in the region where Joseph planned to move his family, and he was afraid to go. God warned Joseph in a dream to move his family to Nazareth because he didn't want Joseph's family to be subject to this evil ruler. Joseph's obedience to this fear enabled Scripture to be fulfilled. God can instill a healthy fear in us to keep us safe and protected. How do you stay obedient to God and be reverent to this kind of fear? Keep the lines of communication open to God. Be in union with Him and one with His Spirit. Become fearless in being one with God.

Day 270: Read Matthew 8:23-27
You of little faith were afraid.

The disciples panicked when a violent storm arose without any warning. They begged Jesus to help them. Even in the very presence of Jesus, His disciples were fearful. Even though they had watched Jesus miraculously heal multitudes of people, they still didn't trust Him to control the wind and the waves. Is there a place in your life that you don't trust God to work in? After the disciples witnessed Jesus rebuke the wind and the waves, they were in awe of His power. God controls and can calm every problem we face when we ask. Become fearless in the asking.

Day 271: Read Matthew 10:17-28
Do not be afraid; everything hidden will be made known.

Jesus warned His disciples that they would experience persecution like He had experienced. He encouraged them not to be afraid of those who could kill the body; rather, He warned to be afraid of the one who could destroy the soul. Jesus encouraged them to keep on speaking and proclaiming the good news. What has the Lord asked you to do that you were fearful at first? How did God help you conquer your fear? God knows everything that happens to us. Even though we may be persecuted now, we will be vindicated later. Become fearless in seeking life-long vindication.

Day 272: Read Matthew 10:29-42
Do not be afraid; you are so valuable to God.

Jesus tells us that God knows everything that happens to one of His children—even to the sparrows that fall. He reminds us that we are far more valuable than a sparrow. To show how much He values us, God knows the very number of hairs on our head. Because God values us so much, we don't need to be afraid when life's daily trials occur. Do you know your value to God? Stand firm in your worth and continue to praise God. Become fearless in knowing your worth to God.

Day 273: Read Matthew 14:1-12
King Herod was afraid of the people.

John the Baptist condemned King Herod for his openly immoral lifestyle that opposed God's laws. Convicted by John's words of condemnation, Herod desired to execute his critic. However, Herod was afraid of the people's acceptance of the well–known prophet. When the opportunity did arise for Herod to have John killed, he became greatly distressed. He no longer wanted him dead, but neither did he want to be embarrassed before his dinner guests. Peer pressure happens at any age to anyone! Herod was afraid of disappointing his guests, and he sought their approval—not God's. Have you ever given into the crowd because you didn't want to be embarrassed by doing right? Christianity is not a popularity contest. Stand out and go against the grain when necessary. The only favor we believers seek comes from God. Become fearless in always doing right.

Day 274: Read Matthew 14:22-33
Jesus told them to take courage and not to be afraid.

Jesus walked on the water toward the boat where the twelve disciples were rowing in the midst of a fierce storm. Peter was the first to see the Savior. Encouraged by Jesus, Peter walked confidently on the water until he took his eyes from Jesus and saw the intensity of the waves and began to sink. Jesus reached out and saved him. Jesus is the only One who can help us. When have you started out faithful and full of energy, only to doubt and become ineffective? When we doubt, we are allowing fear to enter our lives. When we take our eyes off Jesus, we lose focus. Become fearless, and keep your eyes on Jesus.

Day 275: Read Matthew 17:1-13
Jesus touched them and told them to get up and not to be afraid.

Jesus brought Peter, James, and John with Him to the mountain where He was transfigured before God. The experience enabled them to see the appearance of heaven. The disciples saw Moses and Elijah, and Peter told the Lord that he would build shelters for the three. The disciples became terrified at hearing the voice of God and fell face down. In your own willingness to help, have you ever overstepped your boundaries? There is a time to work and a time to worship. Wise people discern the difference and obey. Become fearless in being present in worship.

154

Day 276: Read Matthew 21:23-27
**The religious leaders were afraid of the
people as they tried to trap Jesus.**

While Jesus was teaching in the temple courts, the Pharisees came by and demanded to know where He got the authority to teach. Jesus saw through their plan to trap Him, knowing if He said that His authority came from God, they would cry blasphemy. If Jesus had said by His own authority, the crowds would have declared that the Pharisees had greater authority. So Jesus answered their question with a question about John the Baptist that exposed their true motives. They were afraid of the people and did not answer. Do others try to trip you up in your walk and relationship with Jesus? Remember by whose authority you live your life. God is the same today as He was yesterday and will be tomorrow. He doesn't change. Rest in His assurance. Become fearless resting in the God who doesn't change.

Day 277: Read Matthew 21:33-46
**They looked for a way to arrest Jesus, but
they were afraid of the people.**

The chief priests and the Pharisees never believed that Jesus was who He said He was. They did not believe His story or the authority by which He taught the people. They knew Jesus spoke this parable against them, and they desperately wanted to arrest him but couldn't for fear of His followers. There will always be those who don't believe in Jesus; we are still called to love them anyway. Do you show as much love and compassion to your unbelieving friends and family as you do believers? You may be the only believer who has ever shown them the unconditional love of Jesus. Give your love away—just like Jesus. Become fearless in loving those who don't love Jesus.

Day 278: Read Matthew 26:36-46
Keep watch and pray so that you will not fall into temptation.

Jesus urged His disciples to keep watch and pray, warning them that the spirit was willing, but the body was weak. When we remember to keep watch by praying to God, He infuses us with courage and strength to combat Satan's power. Do you have empowering prayer sessions with God? When we hold nothing back from God and seek Him wholeheartedly in daily prayer, we gain His power. Become fearless in gaining His strength and power through prayer.

Day 279: Read Matthew 27:45-56
The centurion and guards of Jesus saw the truth of their actions and were terrified.

The centurion, a captain in charge of Jesus' execution, and the guards were terrified because they instantaneously knew Jesus was the Son of God. Darkness covered the land, the veil in the temple was torn in two, a violent earthquake convulsed the ground, the dead rose from their graves and walked in Jerusalem. No doubt God had their attention. Seeing the truth of our actions played out in others' lives can be very humbling. Oftentimes, God gives us a second opportunity to right a wrong, but not this time for the guards. Have you wronged someone and need to make right? Today is your opportunity. Make yourself a humble pie and take a bite. Become fearless in righting all your wrongs.

Day 280: Read Matthew 28:1-7
The angel told them not to be afraid because
Jesus had risen just as He said.

The angel had a powerful message for the women and urged them not to be afraid for Jesus was not there. The resurrection brought hope and courage—not fear. The angel urged them to look and see that He was not dead, but living. "Go look for Him in Galilee and tell His disciples the good news." Do you believe in the resurrection of Jesus? The resurrection of the Son of God is the power of God. This very same power is available to those who believe now, as well as on the day of our resurrection. Become fearless in the hope and courage of the resurrection.

Day 281: Read Matthew 28:8-20
Do not be afraid; tell them they
will see me in Galilee.

Jesus appeared to the women and told them not to be afraid, but to continue on and remind the others to meet Him in Galilee. He showed the women and the disciples that everything had happened exactly as He told them it would. We can put our trust in Jesus. He is who He said He was, and He completed everything He promised. Do you trust Jesus to meet you right where you are at in life? When asked, Jesus will meet us on any road of life that we are traveling. Become fearless in trusting Jesus right where you're at.

MARK

Day 282: Read Mark 4:35-41
**Jesus asked His disciples why
they were so afraid.**

The disciples lived with the Lord and had come to know Him and His capabilities, yet when in dangerously high water, they doubted Him. They couldn't see how Jesus could be helpful in their lives. In times of trouble, we often do this too. When have you underestimated the power of Jesus? Rest in His faithfulness to us and harness His power! Become fearless in the power of Jesus.

Day 283: Read Mark 5:25-34
Trembling with fear, she told Him the truth.

Oftentimes we think God is too big, and we can't possibly bother Him with our needs. This account of how God healed the bleeding woman shows us exactly the opposite. Jesus was showing us what true faith looks like. Complete faith in Jesus releases His healing power in our lives. Have you ever felt that a problem has kept you from approaching God? Don't allow any fears to keep you from Him. Come before Him with the truth, and believe He will provide. Become fearless in seeking God's healing power.

Day 284: Read Mark 5: 21-43
Don't be afraid; just believe.

Upon learning his daughter had died, Jairus felt hopeless and afraid. His hope and trust no longer rested in Jesus. When in the midst of our own crisis, we often feel hopeless and afraid too. If we remain bound in our fear, we will miss the miracles, the healings, and the workings of Jesus. When have you lost your hope in Jesus? Listen to Him when He said, "Don't be afraid; just believe." Become fearless in the belief of Jesus.

Day 285: Read Mark 6:45-52
Take courage and don't be afraid.

The disciples were fearful because they thought a ghost was coming near them. When they realized the presence was Jesus, their fears were relieved. Have you ever been in this kind of gripping fear? When we are in fear, we can call on the Lord's name because He is always with us. The mere presence of Jesus or calling on His Holy name removes fear. Christ's presence is always the solution to fear. Become fearless in the presence of the Lord.

Day 286: Read Mark 9:1-13
The disciples were so frightened they were at a loss for words.

For the three disciples to see the glory of God displayed in the whitest white imaginable must have been astonishing. They were so afraid of what they were permitted to see, they were speechless. They feared the divine authority they were seeing and hearing. Do you fear God with this same reverence and awe? One day we will wonder no more about the words we've read and the Bible lessons we've brought to life in our minds. One day we believers will walk in final victory; the old will fade and the new will begin. Jesus Christ lives! Become fearless in seeking the image of the living Christ today.

Day 287: Read Mark 9:30-32
The disciples were afraid to ask.

Jesus had predicted His death for the second time, but His disciples still did not understand. They were too afraid to ask questions. Perhaps because Jesus was a healthy man who was walking with them, they could not understand why He would be talking about His death. Or perhaps the lack of understanding came because He often talked in parables they could not understand. When have you been too afraid to ask a question? We learn by asking questions and thereby step from the darkness into the light. The more questions you ask, the more knowledgeable you'll become. Become fearless in asking questions.

Day 288: Read Mark 10:32-34
Jesus predicted His death a third time, and His followers were afraid.

When Jesus predicted His death and resurrection a third time, His disciples still did not understand and were afraid to ask about it. They only heard Jesus talk about His death and became fixated on the fact that their mighty King would die. The disciples thought they would lose Jesus forever. They couldn't understand the miracle of the resurrection Jesus was attempting to explain. The Old Testament foretold of the coming Messiah, Jesus Christ, His life's purpose, and His death. As soon as Jesus was born, Scripture was fulfilled. Do you know the story of God through Jesus? Read the Bible and watch the life of Jesus unfold from the Old Testament through the New Testament. Become fearless in learning and knowing the life of Jesus Christ.

Day 289: Read Mark 11:1-33
They feared Jesus power and plotted to kill Him.

Jesus made such an entrance into Jerusalem that all the people shouted, *"Hosanna!"* which means "save"! The people recognized Jesus as the Lord who saves. The chief priests and the teachers of law saw the great following Jesus had, and they feared His popularity and power. They had such a fear of Him, they plotted to kill Him. What do you fear or hate that you really don't understand? We live in a world where we often fear what we don't understand. We believers only need to fear God and ask Him to help us understand the rest. When we love the God who saves, we become a product of His unconditional love for all to see. Become fearless in becoming love to others.

Day 290: Read Mark 12:1-17
The religious leaders were afraid of the crowd around Jesus, so they left.

Two groups of people were trying to trick and trap Jesus. The Pharisees, a religious group who were proponents of ritual purity, saw Jesus as a rule breaker and couldn't understand the truths He taught and the miracles He performed. The Herodians, a political group, feared Jesus would cause an uprising and make their city unstable. In this parable, the tenants represent the religious leaders who are ignoring the people they should be leading to God. When Jesus taught this parable, they were afraid of the crowd and left. How much energy do you exert trying to bring something down versus trying to understand it? Be slow to speak, even slower to judge, and quick to understand others. Become fearless in understanding others.

LUKE

Day 291: Read Luke 1:1-17
But the angel told Zechariah not to be afraid.

God gave Zechariah the desire of his heart—a son. God also set in motion the preparations for Jesus to come. Prayers were answered, and Scripture was fulfilled. Although you may not have an angel deliver a vision to you, be open to the unlikely. Be open to the forgotten desires of your heart—the ones you sat and prayed about for years, perhaps thinking they were hopeless. What are the unanswered desires of your heart? Be open to receive what God will give you today. Become fearless in your heart's desire.

Day 292: Read Luke 1:26-37
The angel told Mary not to be afraid.

When God gives us a vision or puts a desire in our heart, cultivate that dream and accept it as truth. God can use anyone to do His work, and Scripture has shown this truth to us. God wants to use you for a very specific purpose; He even created you uniquely for it. Do you know your God-given purpose? If so, what is it? Seek out God's purpose for you. Become fearless in achieving His purpose for your life.

Day 293: Read Luke 2:1-20
The angel told them not to be afraid.

Fear turned to joy as the shepherds in the field realized the value of the gift being shown to them so long ago. They ran, probably at top speed to see the Savior of the world. They were filled with such joy of what God let them see, they spread the word about the birth of Jesus to anyone who would listen. When you finally realized who Jesus is in our own life, how did you respond then? How about now? Never forget the newness of God, and cultivate your joy for Him. Become fearless in your love for God always.

Day 294: Read Luke 5:1-11
Don't be afraid; leave everything behind and follow Him.

When Jesus' disciple, Simon, agreed to let down his nets, a miracle happened. The disciples saw yet again another example of what happens when they trusted and obeyed Jesus. Have you ever said to Jesus, "Because You say so, Lord, I will"? If so, what happened? If not, tell Him today, "Because You say so, Lord, I will!" Realize you need God's help and let down your nets! Leave everything behind and follow Him. Become fearless in letting go and giving into God's direction.

Day 295: Read Luke 8:22-25
In fear they saw Jesus calm the storm.

The disciples were in danger and so feared for their lives in the storm they awakened Jesus to help them. Jesus can calm any storm we go through when we call on His name. He is the Author of creation and controls the world, yet He longs to hear you call His name. Have you ever felt like you had lost all control in this world? Fear not in times of trouble; just call on the name of the Jesus, and He will prevail. Become fearless in times of trouble.

Day 296: Read Luke 8:26-39
They were overcome with fear because of their livelihood.

The people of the region were overcome with fear and asked Jesus to leave because they linked their livelihood to livestock. Jesus had just destroyed their herd of livestock. They couldn't focus on the miracle of Legion's now being in his right mind; they could only focus on the loss of their wealth. What do you value so much in your life that you fear losing? Trust that God is the ultimate Provider and focus on His miracles. Become fearless, and let go what you hold tightly.

Day 297: Read Luke 8: 40-56
Don't be afraid, just believe.

When Jairus learned that his daughter had died, he listened to Jesus' instructions and continued on. He had faith and believed in what Jesus could do. We face all kinds of losses in our lifetime: the loss of a job, the fracturing of a friendship, the death of a loved one. We believers place our trust in Jesus, follow His instructions, and continue on in the face of loss. What loss have you faced in your life? Don't give up; give in to your faith in Jesus. Continue on! Become fearless in your belief in Jesus.

Day 298: Read Luke 9:28-36
They were afraid and questioned the authority of Jesus.

Peter questioned Jesus, asking if it was good for him to be where Jesus led him. The Son of God will never lead us astray. As the ruler of all believers, Jesus has the final word and the last say. When we are given clear direction from Him through His Word, we need to obey without question. When have you been hesitant about going in the direction that Jesus is clearly leading you? Life is hard, and it won't be easy, but don't stray from the directions, lessons, and obedience of following Jesus. Today, make no excuses! Become fearless and follow where Jesus is leading.

Day 299: Read Luke 9:44-45
They were afraid to ask Him about it.

The disciples had missed some key information that Jesus had been giving them because they were too consumed with their own selfish desires. They couldn't hear Jesus because they were too busy hypothesizing which one of them would be the greatest in the kingdom. When have you been so afraid of the direction that Jesus was leading you that you simply abandoned the thought process and continued on in your own selfish desires? Having hard conversations with Jesus may result in going outside of your comfort zone for the kingdom. Don't ignore these promptings! Lean in and pay close attention for hearing Him is how God's will is done on earth. Become fearless in understanding Jesus.

Day 300: Read Luke 12:4-5
Do not be afraid of those who kill the body.

Jesus calls us friends and reminds us very boldly that we are to stand firm in our Christian conviction and fear no one but God. We need not fear those who may temporarily harm us; we need to fear only the one who can eternally harm. Is there a person or a group of people in your life you allow to weaken your witness for Jesus? Speak up as the Holy Spirit permits. Become fearless in your conviction for Christ.

Day 301: Read Luke 12:6-7
Don't be afraid; you are worth far more than many sparrows.

We are valuable to God because He tells us in this Scripture that He cares for all of His creations. When the world evaluates us on how we act and what we look like, God sees our worth. He digs deep and evaluates our hearts. Do you gauge your worth by the opinions of others or by God's opinion? We belong to Him and have incredible value in His eyes. Become fearless knowing your invaluable worth to God.

Day 302: Read Luke 12:22-34
Do not be afraid; your Father is giving you the kingdom.

Jesus tells us not to worry about our life; God has provided for us now, and He will in the kingdom to come. He encourages us to store up treasures in Heaven. These treasures include sharing of our time, talent, and belongings or wealth with others. How can you store up more treasures in Heaven? Hand over all areas of your life to the authority of God. Become fearless in acquiring kingdom treasures.

Day 303: Read Luke 18:1-8
The judge did not care about men or fear God.

In this parable, the widow persistently requests justice and continuously comes before the judge to plead her case. Even though the judge didn't care about men or fear God, he granted the widow her request because of her unceasing persistence. When we petition God with our requests, we need to adopt that same determination. We are not to be repetitious in long, drawn-out prayers; rather, we are to be constant in keeping our requests before Him. About what matter have you been persistent in prayer? Your continued prayers may even affect the non-believer as the widow's persistence affected the heart of the judge. Bring your requests before the Lord daily and expect Him to intervene! Become fearless in persistent prayer.

Day 304: Read Luke 19:11-27
I was afraid of you, Lord.

In this parable, Jesus showed us how to use the resources He has entrusted to us to expand His kingdom. When God trusts us with little, we must honor Him and use the resource well. In so doing, He will trust us with even more next time. We should not be afraid to use our connections, talents or resources our Lord has provided for us. With what has Jesus trusted you? How are you honoring, multiplying, and expanding that trust? No one knows when Jesus will return! Become fearless now in using what God has provided.

Day 305: Read Luke 20:1-19
The teachers of the law were immobilized by fear, and they were afraid of the people.

The teachers and the chief priests were annoyed with Jesus' answers, His authority, and the followers He was attracting. They tried to trap Him into claiming His authority came from God; instead, Jesus told a parable that revealed the truth of what was in their hearts. His answer enraged them, and they looked for another way to arrest Jesus and put an end to Him. However, they were afraid of the people. These teachers of the law and chief priests did not fear God; they only feared men. Who or what in this life do you still fear? The believers of Jesus Christ and keepers of God's law only fear God. The perfect love of God casts out fears. Become fearless in casting out all other fears.

Day 306: Read Luke 21:5-19
When you hear of dangerous times,
do not be frightened.

Jesus warns about times when false teachers will try to deceive us into believing the second coming is now. Only God knows the exact time for the imminent return of His Son. Jesus reminds us that nation will rise against nation, and fearful catastrophes will happen—much like those being seen today. He instructs His believers not to worry or have fear, but to stand firm and gain eternal life. Your life is secured, bought and paid for by Jesus. What do you live in fear of today? Cast your worries and fears onto the One who cares about you. Become fearless without worry or concern in your life.

Day 307: Read Luke 21:10-24
When you hear of wars, do not be fearful;
the end will not come right away.

Jesus warned about nations at war, earthquakes, famine, religious persecution, and all kinds of catastrophic events that will happen. Our Lord told us not to be fearful when these things happen; He will be with us. We will not perish. Standing firm and gaining life is the definition of being fearless. The believers of Jesus Christ can stand firm because they know how the last chapter ends! Peace comes when fear is released. Do you have this kind of peace when thinking about the perilousness of the end times? Jesus died on the Cross to hand this peace and salvation to you as His love offering. Accept the peace of your salvation. God is always with us! Become fearless in resting in His peace.

Day 308: Read Luke 21:25-38
Some will faint in terror of what they see coming.

Jesus briefly describes His return by using the parable of the fig tree to explain that His believers will know when the kingdom of God is near. He encouraged the disciples to be watchful so they could escape the horrible things they will see. They will be able to stand unafraid before God. Rather than be terrified, we believers have already been told of the future to come. Even though we patiently await the Messiah's return, we still have work to be done in the waiting time. How do you remain watchful for God's kingdom? In what work do you engage while you wait? Keep watchful, pray without ceasing, and praise Him while waiting the day of His return. Come, Lord Jesus, we're waiting! Become fearless in the wait.

Day 309: Read Luke 22:1-71
They were searching for a way to get rid of Jesus because they were afraid of the people.

The crowds were increasing daily, and the Passover was sure to draw even more people to Jesus. The only obstacle the religious leaders feared was the crowds who followed Jesus. They feared a backlash if they laid a hand on Jesus publically. The teachers of the law and the chief priests needed to confront Jesus in private—out of the public eye and scrutiny. They were delighted when Judas came to them to betray Jesus. The false disciple agreed to hand Jesus over to them when no crowds were present. Have you ever done things out of the public eye for fear of what others might think of you? God sees things done in the darkness as well as in the daylight. He even knows our thoughts before we think them. Become fearless in hiding nothing from God.

Day 310: Read Luke 23:1-56
"Don't you fear God?" one criminal
asked the other.

Jesus was being crucified between two criminals. One criminal mocked Him while the other believed in Him. The believer asked the other criminal if he feared God. The one who believed asked Jesus to be remembered in His paradise. Even while Jesus is entering the bonds of death, He is still helpful and grants eternal life to the repentant criminal who asks and accepts Him. God is the giver and taker of life. If we accept Him and the salvation He offers, He is the extender of life on the new earth. Do you know why you fear God? We believers know God is the living offer of eternal life. Become fearless in the reality of God as the giver and taker of life.

Day 311: Read Luke 24:1-12
In their fright the women bowed their
faces low to the ground.

Showing proper reverence to God is bowing our heads low to respect His authority. When these women saw what must have looked like a vision from God, they immediately bowed down to the gleaming white visions of angels. The two angels reminded the women of Jesus' words about His death and resurrection; they remembered and ran off to share the news with the disciples. How has God appeared to you and reminded you of His words? Believers show their reverence to God when they love and obey His Word and submit all they are to His authority. Become fearless in showing reverence to God.

Day 312: Read Luke 24:13-53
The disciples were frightened by what they saw.

While the two disciples were still talking about the appearance of Jesus on the walk to Emmaus, Jesus appeared in their midst, frightening them. He encouraged them to touch His hands and feet to see that He was indeed alive. Seeing that Jesus was alive and completely immortal reminded the disciples that one day they would also be gathered by Him and have eternal life. The death and resurrection of Jesus was difficult for His disciples to understand—even with the proof standing before their own eyes. Have you ever been in disbelief or frightened by what God has allowed you to see? Ask God for understanding, and He will provide. God has a purpose for everything under the sun. Jesus came to fulfil the Scripture as the love offering for all. Become fearless in understanding what God allows you to see.

JOHN

Day 313: Read John 6:16-21
Jesus told the terrified disciples not to be afraid.

When the storm struck the boat filled with disciples, they trembled in fear from the ferocity of the wind and the waves, as well as from seeing Jesus walk on the water. Even though these disciples walked with Jesus and saw Him perform many miracles, they were still frightened and did not expect Him to show up and rescue them. Great things happen when Jesus shows up! When did you least expect Him, and He was there? Diligently seek Him; He's always by your side. Do not be afraid of the things He will let you see. Become fearless in expecting Jesus to show up.

173

Day 314: Read John 9:1-41
The blind man's parents were afraid of the Jews.

After Jesus healed the blind man's vision, the religious Jewish leaders did not believe it and sent for the blind man's parents. The parents were afraid of the Jews and made their son give an account of his ability to see. When we are in fear, we often look for a way out instead of stepping right into fear with the confidence Jesus gives us. They were fearful because anyone who acknowledged the miracles of Jesus and professed He indeed was the Christ would be put out of the synagogue. When in fear how have you looked for a way out? Stop looking for a way out and acknowledge the confidence of Jesus, who is always by your side. Take that step right into fear. He's rooting for you! Become fearless in walking in fear.

Day 315: Read John 12:12-36
Do not be afraid; your King is coming.

Just as Zechariah 9:9 prophesied that a king would ride into Jerusalem on a colt, this passage records the fulfillment of Zechariah's prophecy as Jesus rides into the city on a young donkey. Many prophecies of the Old Testament came to life in the New Testament. This prophecy was fulfilled, and so will the prophecy of the second coming of Jesus. Our King will return. Jesus died to give everyone who believed eternal life. He will back again; are you ready? Become fearless in sharing the prophecy of the King's return.

Day 316: Read John 14:15-31
**Do not be afraid; I do not give to you
as the world gives.**

This passage is the introduction of the Holy Spirit—another Counselor and Comforter—to the disciples. Jesus tells His disciples that the Counselor will be with them forever and will help them remember His teachings. Where Jesus is going His disciples cannot go. Through the Counselor, they will remember His lessons and have His peace amongst the chaos of life. The peace Jesus left for us remains in our hearts through the indwelling Holy Spirit. Will you ask the Counselor to guide your life and rest in God's peace? Go after and seek in prayer the peace that Jesus gives. Become fearless in seeking God's peace.

Day 317: Read John 19:1-16
Pilate was distressed and afraid.

Pilate had Jesus flogged to appease the people, but that beating wasn't enough. They wanted more. He again appealed to the Jewish people, stating he had found no wrong committed by Jesus. He then presented the beaten Jesus to them. The people still yelled for Him to be crucified. Pilate answered the crowd again by stating there were no charges against Jesus. The Jews fired back that anyone claiming to be the Son of God must die. Pilate then retreated inside of his palace even more afraid. Do you think Pilate was more afraid of the people or of God? When we're under intense pressure, we believers need to remember to fear God only—not people. Become steadfast in difficult decisions. Become fearless under pressure.

Day 318: Read John 19:17-42
Before Jesus' death, Joseph was a secret disciple because of his fearfulness.

The life of Jesus changed many people, but His death left an indelible impact on our lives and declared a call to action. Before Jesus' death, Joseph was a secret disciple who believed but wouldn't admit it publicly because of his Jewish position in the community. After witnessing His death and the power of God, Joseph boldly walked into Pilate's office and asked for Jesus' body to give Him a proper burial. He no longer cared about the things of the past; he only cared that he was a believer and became a man of action. How has Jesus' death changed your life? How have you been called into action? Be bold today! Become fearless in His call to action for your life.

Day 319: Read John 20:19-23
The disciples gathered behind locked doors for fear of the Jews.

After Jesus was crucified and raised from the grave, He appeared before His beloved disciples. Jesus' disciples watched everything that had been done to Him over the last few days and feared what the Jews would do next. They stayed behind locked doors until Jesus appeared and gave them the authority to be bold again. Fear immobilizes us and keeps us from doing what we want to do. Jesus stood among His disciples, told them He was sending them out, and breathed the Holy Spirit over them as their guide. Could you imagine what it would have been like to have been one of His disciples in the room when He appeared? Just as Jesus breathed the Holy Spirit into commission for His disciples, He breathes the same authority and spirit unto His believers today. As His Father sent Him, Jesus sends you! Become fearless in using God's authority.

ACTS

Day 320: Read Acts 2:22-40
The Lord is at my right hand; I will not be shaken.

David had no fear because he knew the Lord was always with him. Peter is addressing the crowd with examples and life proofs that Jesus has risen from the grave, which indeed is good news for them to accept. He gave an example of David who prophesized the Messiah's resurrection, and in David's words, he found solace. David became fearless because His future was already determined for him and his ascending to the throne. Realizing only God can save us, what part of your future are you controlling? Give your life—your past, your present, and your future—to God. Hold nothing back! Become fearless in the resurrection of Christ.

Day 321: Read Acts 5:1-11
Great fear seized the whole church.

Ananias and his wife, Sapphira, thought they could find a way around the laws of God. In doing so, they lied and tested the Holy Spirit. Their actions were wrong, and their death-sentence punishment for their sins caused great fear to spread through the entire church. We believers are not exempt from Satan's tempting. How does Satan try to make you stumble? Let nothing slip you up. Remember God is holy and so are His people. Become fearless in your honesty with others and especially with the Lord.

Day 322: Read Acts 5:12:42
The captain and his officers feared
the people more than God.

God had a job for the apostles. An angel of the Lord opened the jail doors so the apostles could go into the temple square and teach the people. When the captain and his officers found out, they did not use force to stop the apostles from teaching because they feared the people would stone them. They feared the wrath of the people more than God. Peter and the other apostles feared only God—not men. When God calls us to do something He makes a way for us to do it. How has God opened a previously closed and locked door for you? We believers fear God only. Remain fearless in the task He's given and complete it. Expect God to show up and make a way! Become a fearless, unstoppable disciple of God.

Day 323: Read Acts 7:1-53
When God spoke, Moses trembled
with fear and did not look.

Stephen, one of the first deacons, delivered a historical speech about Israel's relationship with God. He spoke of how Moses was used mightily by God. When an angel appeared before Moses in the flames of a burning bush, he was amazed at the sight. Then he trembled with fear and did not dare open his eyes when he heard the voice of God. The Lord instructed Moses to take off his sandals for he was standing on holy ground. One day when your eyes are finally opened and you stand before Jesus, what will you see? We believers can enter the presence of God any time we want through prayer, service, or reading our Bibles. God is waiting for you! Become fearless in seeking Him on His holy ground.

178

Day 324: Read Acts 9:1-31
They were all afraid of Saul.

Saul was a zealous murderer of people who had been converted and had followed the way of Jesus. For the disciples to believe that Saul had changed was not easy, and they were all afraid and doubted him. How God uses His people is always amazing. He even pursues those who persecute Him in an attempt to win their heart. How God uses recovering sinners regardless of the life they once lived is also amazing. Do you allow your testimony for Jesus to be easily seen or heard? Speak boldly in the name of the Lord. Tell all what He has done in your life. Become fearless in your testimony about Jesus Christ.

Day 325: Read Acts 10:1-48
**God accepts men from every nation
who fear Him.**

Though Cornelius and his family did not know God, they feared Him. In this Scripture passage, God sent Peter to share the gospel with them. God provides a way for all those seeking Him to become believers. Even now every nation has people who are ready to hear the gospel of Jesus Christ. With whom is God asking you to share the Gospel? Spend time rehearsing the Gospel of Jesus, who He was, what He has done, and how He is working through you. This is the matter of eternal life in heaven versus an everlasting, agonizing death in hell. Become fearless in sharing the Gospel.

Day 326: Read Acts 13:1-52
Some did not accept the truth and stirred up trouble for the God-fearing women.

Through the efforts of Paul and Barnabas, the Jewish people heard the message of God. Many believed and were converted when the truth reached their ears. When others heard the truth of God, they ran from it and created trouble within God's community. When Paul and Barnabas were expelled from the area, they simply shook the dust from their sandals and the joy of the Lord filled their hearts. When confronted with the truth of your own actions, don't run away; allow the truth to adjust your life. How do you keep the truth of God in your everyday life? Hold onto the truth, adjust your life to match, and be full of joy in the Lord. Become fearless in keeping the truth in your life.

Day 327: Read Acts 16:16-40
The jailer fell trembling as he realized the power of God.

The jailer who was keeping watch over Paul and Silas in prison was awakened by the violently shaking foundation of the prison. The jailer saw that the prison doors had been opened. When he saw that the prisoners' chains had been undone, he fell to the ground trembling because he had seen the miraculous power of God firsthand. The jailer saw his own need for a Savior, and he also knew he'd be held responsible for any prisoner's escape. He risked it all to know the truth and how to be saved. What have you risked to follow Jesus? The joy you receive from the Lord far outweighs the risk. The reward that is awaiting those who believe is indescribable. The risk and the reward is around the corner; keep going! Become fearless in risking it all for the gospel of Jesus Christ.

Day 328: Read Acts 18:1-17
Do not be afraid; keep on speaking.

The Lord's call for us to be His mouthpiece comes with an abundance of responsibility. People often don't like to hear the good news because it usually means that they will have to change the way they live in one way or another. They see the personal work they need to do—not the blessing and freedom that come from hearing the good news. The Lord told Paul to keep speaking on His behalf and to look for the people of the city who believe. Have strength knowing you're not alone. Do you have a community of friends who are following Jesus? Ask God to lead you to them like He led Paul. Keep on speaking! Become fearless in finding God's people.

Day 329: Read Acts 19:1-20
They were all seized with fear.

In this passage a group of Jews had been traveling from place to place driving out demons and calling on the deity being worshipped in the place where they were working. In this particular place, they used the name of Jesus Christ and Paul without even knowing them. God only gives His power to those who personally know and believe in Him. Since this group did not know God, their demon overpowered them and beat them. When the rest of the Jews and Greeks saw their deception exposed, the people were seized with fear upon seeing the power of God and how His power is only granted to His followers. In what area has God given you His power? Become fearless in the power that God has given you.

Day 330: Read Acts 23:1-11
The commander was afraid Paul would be torn to pieces from the violent debate.

Paul deflected the conflict from his message to the controversy of the religious leaders who surrounded him. The controversial debate was about the resurrection of the body at death. The Sadducees did not believe in the resurrection of the body, and the Pharisees did. The debate became so violent that the commander sent the troops to remove Paul for fear he would be torn apart. Have you ever witnessed an intense argument about the Bible? How did you determine who was right? When we spend time learning and studying the Word of God, He gifts believers with the wisdom of the Holy Spirit. Then when the time comes and we are under pressure for our faith, the Holy Spirit provides us with the power to stand up and answer boldly. Become fearless in speaking boldly about your faith in Jesus.

Day 331: Read Acts 24:1-27
Felix was afraid and wanted to hear no more.

Paul's presentation of the gospel to Felix hit a nerve on his lack of self-control and righteous living, scaring the Roman governor of Judea. In his past, Felix had been an adulterer and was afraid of the coming judgment. He didn't want to hear anymore from Paul. Oftentimes when we share the gospel, people who are living in sin and come under the conviction of the Holy Spirit may react in much the same way as Felix when they hear the truth. We don't get to control how people react when hearing the gospel. We do have the obligation given by God to share the gospel when led by the Holy Spirit. Be ready to speak truth. Become fearless in sharing the gospel without regard for reactions.

Day 332: Read Acts 27:1-26
Do not be afraid; God will lead the way.

God was with Paul and spoke to him in the vision of an angel, who told the apostle that He would get him out of his perilous situation. God encouraged him and said that all who sailed with him would be spared. Because one man believed, the lives of many were saved. As a follower of Jesus, we too are influencing others, both near and far. In what area of your life has God told you to keep going and not to be afraid? God always goes before those who believe in Him, leading the way. He's got you! Become fearless knowing God is with you wherever you go.

Day 333: Read Acts 27:27-44
Fearing their ship would be smashed against the rocks, they prayed to God.

Paul was a prisoner on a ship sailing toward Rome when the crew realized they were nearing land. They dropped anchors, checked sea depths, and prayed to God for daylight. When in crisis, we need to use all of the skills we've been given and continue to pray to God for His help. Seeking God's help is not an all or nothing; it's an all and everything, including prayer. We need to do all we can do, and then trust God to do His part. Do you pray to God when life is good, or do you pray to Him in life's storms? There's no one better to help us with life than the One who created it. Include Him! Become fearless in praying always to God.

ROMANS

Day 334: Read Romans 8:12-27
You did not receive a spirit that makes you fear; you received the Spirit of God.

We who believe are privileged children of God. We have titles of glory to come. We did not receive a spirit of fear but one of adoption, privilege, and responsibility. We are no longer victims to the unbelief that is accompanied by fear. We live in truth and are welcomed by God as His children. Do you live as a child of God without fear? Have no fear, you are His! Become fearless living in your God-ordained role of being His child.

Day 335: Read Romans 11:11-24
Be afraid; God does not spare the unbelievers.

In Paul's message to the Christian Gentiles, he described the difference between faith and salvation by using roots and branches. The Jews had the faith of their heritage, and their branches were broken off because of their unbelief. Their hearts were far from God, and they couldn't rely on heritage for salvation. The Gentiles were the personified shoots of the wild olives that had been grafted in because of their belief in God. A warning is given by God not to be arrogant about being grafted in, but to be afraid. God did not spare the natural branches and will not spare the unbelievers. Do you depend on the religion of your parents or family heritage? Salvation in Jesus is a one-on-one relationship that no one else can graft you into. If the root is holy, then the branch is holy. Take root! Become fearless in sinking your roots deep into learning the Bible.

1 CORINTHIANS

Day 336: Read 1 Corinthians 2:1-16
I came to you in weakness and fear.

Paul came to the people as an open book. He was guided by the Holy Spirit and was vulnerable for their behalf and trust. He delivered the message of the gospel in its simplicity. He didn't overwhelm his audience or teach them everything he knew about Jesus. He delivered the gospel in its entirety as a vulnerable man who needs God. Have you ever been overwhelmed by a person's knowledge of the Lord? Studying the Word of God for ourselves is so important, and our job includes delivering the plain and simple gospel message to others. Keep it short and simple! Become fearless in your understanding of the gospel and share the simple plan of salvation with others.

Day 337: Read 1 Corinthians 16:1-18
See to it that Timothy has nothing to fear
while he is with you.

Timothy was working for God, and Paul encouraged the people of Corinth to care for his needs while he was there. When we tithe to the church, God uses and multiplies our token ten percent for many different purposes. One important purpose is to pay and care for the clergy or workers of the Light. Our pastors, staff, and missionaries count on God's faithful believers to obey His laws and tithe. Do you give your ten percent tithe or beyond to the church? Start making a way today to cheerfully give the ten percent or beyond for the Lord's work. Time is fleeting. Become fearless in tithing in full.

2 CORINTHIANS

Day 338: Read 2 Corinthians 5:1-21
Because we know what it means to fear the Lord, we persuade others.

The fear of the Lord is the only healthy fear to have. Fearing the Lord helps us want to obey and please Him. All—believers and unbelievers—will stand before God to give an account for their lives—both the good things and the bad. Because we believers know and understand the severity of this accounting, we fear the Lord and try to tell others about our faith in Jesus. Salvation brings a life of freedom, where the old self is gone and only the new remains. How do you persuade others to hear the truth of Jesus? God is for us! Become fearless in persuading others through truth.

Day 339: Read 2 Corinthians 7:1-16
They were all obedient, receiving him with fear and trembling.

Paul shares how God comforts us in our times of fear. He also described two kinds of sorrow that result from sin: worldly sorrow and godly sorrow. Paul says that worldly sorrow is when people are sorry about the effects of their sin actions in the world, which brings death. Godly sorrow for our sins leads to changed behaviors, which leads to repentance and eternal salvation. Paul was delighted and joyful with the Corinthian people's response to his criticism. He was glad his strong words of truth led to repentance. Have you ever received harsh feedback from family, friends, or employer? Take their observations as an opportunity to repent, grow, change, and become better. Because we revere and fear God, we obey and repent. Welcome the feedback and grow! Become fearless in the criticism of others.

Day 340: Read 2 Corinthians 10:1-18
I did not mean to frighten you with my letters.

God has given every believer the tools he or she needs for doing battle without fear. Paul reminds us of this as he defends the authority and power given to him by God to preach the good news to the Corinthians. As believers, we do not wage war as the world does. We win our battles by petitioning God in prayer, placing our hope and trust in Him, spending time in His Word, following the Holy Spirit's promptings, and simply loving others. The Bible reminds us that these weapons arm us in the battle against evil. Which God-given weapons have you perfected? Which ones need work? Get ready for battle! Become fearless in perfecting your weapons.

Day 341: Read 2 Corinthians 11:1-6
I am afraid that just as Eve was deceived, you will also be led astray.

Speaking from his heart, Paul warned the Corinthians not to be deceived by false doctrine or false spirits. Eve was distracted and deceived in the garden of Eden by Satan, and Paul feared the same deception for them. He continued to encourage them to keep Jesus first in their daily lives. What distractions in your life keep you from making Jesus a first priority? Life gets busy, complicated, and confusing, but we need to calm the noise and keep our number-one commitment to follow, obey, and love Jesus. Seek Him! Become fearless in keeping Jesus first.

Day 342: Read 2 Corinthians 12:11-21
**I am afraid I may not find you
as I want you to be.**

Paul wrote to the Corinthians about his concerns and fears for them. He feared they were becoming like the non-believers surrounding them. He sternly warned them in his letters to start living right before he arrived. As believers, we must live our lives in obedience to God. Making this choice will look much different than how the world lives. Do you blend in with the world? Start standing out today. Don't let the world dilute your belief in Jesus. Let the world notice Jesus through you. Become fearless in taking a stand in the world through Jesus.

GALATIANS

Day 343: Read Galatians 2:1-10
Paul feared he was running his race in vain.

Paul spoke the truth to others and honored the gospel that had been given to him. Oftentimes, speaking the truth, especially to others and those who oppose isn't easy. When have you had a difficult conversation? Did you choose to speak truth? The truth honors God. Don't avoid conversations for fear of disagreements. Let others know your heart and speak from it. Become fearless in speaking the truth.

Day 344: Read Galatians 2:11-21
Peter was afraid of those who belonged.

Paul publically confronted Peter for compromising the Gospel for the sanctity of peace. Paul didn't speak to or write to others or other churches about this important issue. He spoke face-to-face with Peter, the one with whom he had a problem. Have you ever had a problem with someone and spoke to everyone about the matter but the person involved? Have you ever compromised the truth of the gospel for peace or to compromise with others? The Bible warns that giving place to slander or gossip in the church body is dangerous ground! Become fearless in addressing your problems head on.

Day 345: Read Galatians 4:1-20
I fear for you unbelievers.

Fearing for others means understanding the wrath of God and what it means not to be known by Him. Because of our belief in Jesus and our relationship with Him, we no longer need to fear the wrath of God. We believers are now called the sons and the daughters of God. Who in your life has turned back to follow the laws of man and not God? Plead with them for their benefit. Become fearless in the work of Christ.

EPHESIANS

Day 346: Read Ephesians 6:5-9
Obey God with fear and sincerity of heart.

In the Bible, many slaves became Christians and experienced freedom in Jesus. Paul describes the kind of heart a slave and a master should have. Slaves and masters alike should obey Christ with a sincere heart of reverence and fear of offending Him. A sincere heart is one that doesn't change with the scenery but does what is right for the sake of it—not for praise or approval. We can apply this type of reverence to our life with God who has authority and power over us. Do you obey God with a sincere heart or only when others are watching? Serve God wholeheartedly because He doesn't rank His people. We are all His favorites. Obey Him with a sincere heart. Become fearless in doing right for the sake of it.

Day 347: Read Ephesians 6:10-20
Pray for me that I may fearlessly declare
the mystery of the gospel.

As the apostle Paul wrote from prison, he didn't ask for prayers to change his situation. He asked only for prayers that he would be able to continue speaking fearlessly for the Lord, encouraging others, and sharing the gospel boldly. God can use us right where we are to share the gospel. With whom could you have a conversation about the hope you have in Jesus? In the perimeter God has given you, tell everyone you can about the story of God. Become fearless in declaring the mystery of the gospel of God.

PHILIPPIANS

Day 348: Read Philippians 1:12-30
Because of my situation, others gained encouragement and became fearless.

Paul continued to minister while in chains, speaking from prison and never giving up as he encouraged others. Those who saw him were encouraged by his words and actions, resulting from his great faith. Everyone is watching our actions as believers. Give them something to really talk about! Every time you praise God wholeheartedly in times of trouble and suffering, others will see Jesus. How do you turn a difficult situation into a worthwhile one? Don't forget in times of trouble that God is always with us, and we can make lemonade out of life's lemons. Become fearless in using every situation allowed by God for His glory.

Day 349: Read Philippians 2:12-18
Shine brightly and work out your salvation with fear and trembling.

Paul was encouraging the congregation of believers to continue to work out their salvation in his absence and to keep going in their "Jesus journey." Life is full of busy activities that can sidetrack our attention daily. As believers, we must be careful where we give our attention and spend our time. Our walk with the Lord is a daily—not just on Sundays when we receive God's message through another. Church is every day. How do you keep your daily focus on the Lord? Don't get sidetracked in life; even the good things of life will try to sidetrack you, occupy your time, and diminish your devotion to God. Shine brightly until He returns! Become fearless in being devoted to God daily.

1 THESSALONIANS

Day 350: Read 1 Thessalonians 3:1-13
Paul was afraid that his efforts were useless.

Paul longed to see the Thessalonian people and hoped and prayed that they didn't fall prey to the Tempter. Satan has the power to tempt both the physical and spiritual body. God's people gain strength knowing Jesus conquered death and Satan in His finished work on the Cross. When we remain obedient to Christ through hardships and temptations, we gain strength, character, and greater compassion for others. How do you remain obedient when tempted? Choose Jesus again each day! Become fearless in temptations.

HEBREWS

Day 351: Read Hebrews 2:5-18
**Jesus broke the fear of death for
all who believe in Him.**

Jesus, God in the flesh, broke through death and destroyed the Enemy who instills fear. We no longer need to live our lives in fear. Jesus made a way for us through His own death and resurrection. He freed us from fear and invites us to live for Him. Do you dread death or do you dream of the great victory that awaits you? When we believe in Jesus, we know death is not final, and hope is not lost! Become fearless in your death which leads to eternal life.

Day 352: Read Hebrews 11:23-40
Through faith they were not afraid of the king's law.

Faith in God helps us see beyond this life. When we trust in God, His perfect will for our lives is completed. God created each one of us for a unique and conquering purpose. Moses' parents knew that God had a special purpose for their son. They became fearless because they trusted that God would protect and care for their child. As a man, Moses did not fear man and continued to live by faith. Faith is letting go of control, handing it over to God and trusting in the things we cannot see. Do you trust God and walk by faith? His way is best! Become fearless in giving God control.

Day 353: Read again Hebrews 11:24-29
By faith Moses did not fear the king's anger.

Faith in God is easily seen in others. Not only did Moses' parents trust God with their son's life, Moses also trusted God, and endured harsh treatments from others. He gave up his pleasures, treasures, and great wealth to do the work and will of the Lord. The Lord used Moses because of his great faith. The sacrifices we make now to do the Lord's work will be given to us later. Moses did not fear the consequences of his actions in this life because he was following God. What could you give up today to become fearless with your own life? Let go of your life to really live it! Become fearless in living for God.

Day 354: Read Hebrews 12:18-29
Moses was trembling with fear.

Moses trembled with fear at the thought of approaching God. Today, every believer can confidently come before Him. Jesus made the difference in how we interact with God. We have Jesus the Mediator to stand between man and God. Through Jesus' life and death on the Cross, God now welcomes us. We do not need to tremble with fear like Moses did. We can be confident in the work that Jesus has already done on our behalf. Yes, we still fear God, but can come to Him through our relationship with Jesus. What is your confident prayer of becoming completely fearless? Every believer is a part of His unshakable kingdom. Come before Him with gratitude and praise! Become fearless in praying to God.

Day 355: Read Hebrews 13:1-7
The Lord is my helper; I will not be afraid.

The Lord is our helper and provider. He will never leave us or forsake us. The Lord can and will fulfill all of our needs. When we learn to be content with what He has already given us, we will not be afraid or fearful of doing without. What has the Lord provided for you in the past? What do you trust He will give you? The Lord is our great Helper! Become fearless in being content with what He provided.

1 PETER

Day 356: Read 1 Peter 2:13-25
Love believers, fear God, and honor the king.

Peter explained the importance of loving believers, fearing God, and honoring our governing authorities. We are commanded to obey God—not man. In this passage, Peter is stating that when we obey governing authorities we are obeying God. God is the One who places men and women in their positions of power and authority. Does knowing this chain of command change your view of local and federal governments? Does the chain of command make a difference in the way you view those in power and ruling in foreign governments? Obey God's laws and those He places in power. Become fearless in honoring all governing authorities.

Day 357: Read 1 Peter 3:8-22
Do not fear what they fear, and do not be frightened.

No one can harm us when we are eager to do good. Those who follow Jesus are set apart and different. We do not repay evil with evil, slander others, and add insults to injury. We call out conflict before it arises. We bring it to the open and try to restore peace. We do not need to fear what others fear because we have God the giver of peace who shows us how to bring peace to others. How do you live peacefully with one another or resolve conflict? Pass the peace! Become fearless in being a peacemaker.

2 PETER   *Day 358: Read 2 Peter 2:1-22*
Some are not afraid of God, and the blackest
darkness is reserved for them.

Peter saw false teachers in his day, and these bold and arrogant people who are not afraid of God can be found today. They blaspheme about matters they do not understand, they mock God, and they gather others to join in their heresy. These false teachers deny the teachings of Jesus. They live their lives answering to no one, but the time is coming when they will find out how the story ends. The blackest darkness is reserved for false teachers and those like them on judgment day. False teachers are everywhere, and their destruction leaves a devastating path. How do you combat the false teachers in your life? Study the Bible, know it, love it, and live it out in your life. Become fearless in standing firm against those who are not afraid of God.

1 JOHN   *Day 359: Read 1 John 4:7-18*
There is no fear in love because fear
is punishment, and love is not.

God is love. If perfect love drives out fear, then we need have no fear if we have God. Fear is a form of punishment. To fear is a burden placed on us by Satan, who is a liar, thief, and a murderer. On the other hand, there is no fear in love because God's perfect love drives out all fear. God is over Satan. In the final judgment where punishments will be handed out, God wins and Satan loses. One day we will stand waiting for judgment before Jesus and give an account for the life we lived. Since we are in God and He is in us, we have no fear. We have been saved from punishment. What a day of jubilation with no more pain, suffering, or sin. Now we will see Jesus face-to-face. Do you have the love of God in you and you in Him? If you have God, you have perfect love. And where perfect love exits, fear does not. Relax in God's love! Become fearless in His perfect love.

Day 360: Read 1 John 4:18-21
The one who fears is not made perfect in God's love.

God's perfect love spreads. We can't know God and not have love running through us; His love is a gift from Him. We are able to love others because we are so loved by Him. If we wholeheartedly love God, we cannot also hate others. Whoever loves God must also love all the people that He created. If we have hate in us, we are liars and did not accept God's love. Every believer is an extension of God; He is able to love others through every believer. We do not get to decide whom we love or hate; we are to love everyone—just like God. His love squelches our fears and shows us how to love and not to hate. What is it exactly that keeps you from loving someone as God loves you? Remember, He forgave you from all of your sins and transgressions against Him. He is only asking that you do the same. Go all out in love! Become fearless in loving others in God's perfect love.

JUDE

Day 361: Read Jude 17-25
Show mercy mixed with fear.

When Jude wrote about *"showing mercy mixed with fear,"* he was describing a healthy way to reverence God. After all, God is the only One we should fear. Through this fear, we have the responsibility to do our God-given job of witnessing to unbelievers. God's request of us should not be taken lightly. How can you get over your fear of sharing who God is with others? Deliver the truth and mercy of Jesus! Become fearless to snatch the unbeliever from the fire.

REVELATION

Day 362: Read Revelation 1:1-20
Do not be afraid, I am the One who holds the keys of life and death.

The apostle John was troubled about the persecution of the Christian church. He was living in exile, refusing to stop preaching the message of God when Jesus appeared to him to reassure him and predict the future of the churches. When John saw the vision of Jesus, he fell at His feet. Jesus is the key to life now and life eternal, and He alone holds the keys to death. We believers realize Jesus is the key to everything, and everything is under His control. How much of your life are you still controlling? When we give control back to God, we accept Him in our lives and have His peace and security. Become fearless in giving up control of our lives to God.

Day 363: Read Revelation 2:1-17
Do not be afraid of what you will suffer.

The believers of Jesus Christ will experience pain and suffering caused by Satan, who roams the earth causing chaos. God even tells us that we will suffer in this life. Our sufferings will come at different times and in different ways, and no one is exempt from the trials of life. God also goes on to tell us that those who remain faithful through trials and suffering will receive a crown that will last—eternal life. In this life we may go from trial to trial and experience great suffering, but eternal life brings no more suffering. How do you draw closer to the Lord in times of suffering? Be faithful—no matter what trial you face. Choose God and keep your eye on the prize! Become fearless in life's trials.

Day 364: Read Revelation 14:1-20
Fear God, and give Him all the glory
for the time of harvest has come.

In the harvest of the earth, the Scripture will be fulfilled as the gospel will be preached to every nation. The first angel will declare the eternal gospel to the rest of the people on earth who haven't yet heard the message of salvation. The angel will announce the time of judgment has come and for people to accept and repent now. The second angel will declare God's enemies (those who didn't follow Satan, but also did not follow God) will now pay for what they've done. The third angel will declare in a loud voice that those who worship the beast (Satan) will now experience God's fury. By now everyone has had the chance to fear God and give Him glory. Essentially, the angels are declaring, "Times up! The harvest will begin!" Do you share the gospel with fervor, knowing you are in a life–or-death situation? Through you, allow God to reach those who might not get the chance to know about Him. Give God all the glory when you're talking with others. Before time runs out, share God's message as the Holy Spirit guides. Become fearless in sharing the gospel.

Day 365: Read Revelation 15:1-8
Who will not fear and glorify the Lord's name?

The vision John revealed describes God's people joining together in song and praising God for the final deliverance from all evil. What a glorious and joyful time to see all evil about to come to an end! The angels' shining clothing was further proof that we will be free from all evils and injustice. Then God's wrath and punishment will begin. Those who do not fear God will not belong, but those who do will join in song. Can you imagine millions of harps joining with millions of voices to praise God in a final victory? The time will come when all will fear the name of the Lord. Become fearless in knowing your day of deliverance is coming.

Epilogue

Step Through Fear

While I was writing this book, it became very clear to me that what we spend our time thinking about—our hopes and our big and little dreams—is where God is already waiting for us to show up. He's planted the passion, and He's just waiting for us to step forward through fear and go with Him into the greatest adventure the two of you will have yet.

I spend a lot of my time thinking about how, when, and where I can proclaim God's goodness and share the gospel. Using the gift He's given me, I encourage others on social media, through my books, and even at the grocery store. When I wonder if I am living out the purpose and passion that God has for my life, I just think about what my grave marker will say, and then I know for sure I'm doing it right.

My marker won't be engraved with "Sandy Holly, Wife, Daughter, Friend to all." It will read Sandy Holly *"asked everyone she knew to read the Bible."* Even in death I want to keep spreading the Word of God for anyone walking by to know how important reading the Bible is. God can operate in and through us when we use the gifts He has given us and act according to His plan for our lives. He's planted the seed. About what do you spend your time dreaming? What will your marker say? Step through your fear and show up; He'll show you what to do next!

She is clothed with strength and dignity,
and she laughs **without fear** of the future.
Proverbs 31:25

About the Author

Sandy Holly and her husband James live in the heart of Virginia. Sandy is passionate about reading, studying, and proclaiming the Word of God, and that is why her Christian company, *Jesus Freak Apparel,* is a proud supporter of Compassion International and Klove Christian radio. Compassion International releases children from poverty around the world in Jesus' name. Klove provides positive and encouraging stories from other Christians and inspiring music through Christian radio, which is broadcast around the world for all to hear about Jesus. Ten percent of every purchase is passed along to these organizations. To learn more, please visit Sandy's online store at JesusFreakApparel.com and learn how your purchase promotes the good news for all to hear.

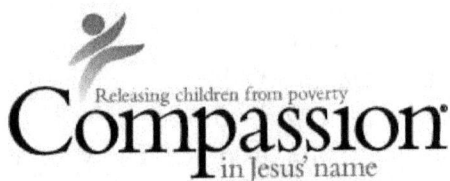

Compassion — Releasing children from poverty in Jesus' name

Recovering Sinner, Adopted By Christ, Saved By Grace — JESUS FREAK — JesusFreakApparel.com

POSITIVE, ENCOURAGING K-LOVE

Read about Sandy's Testimony

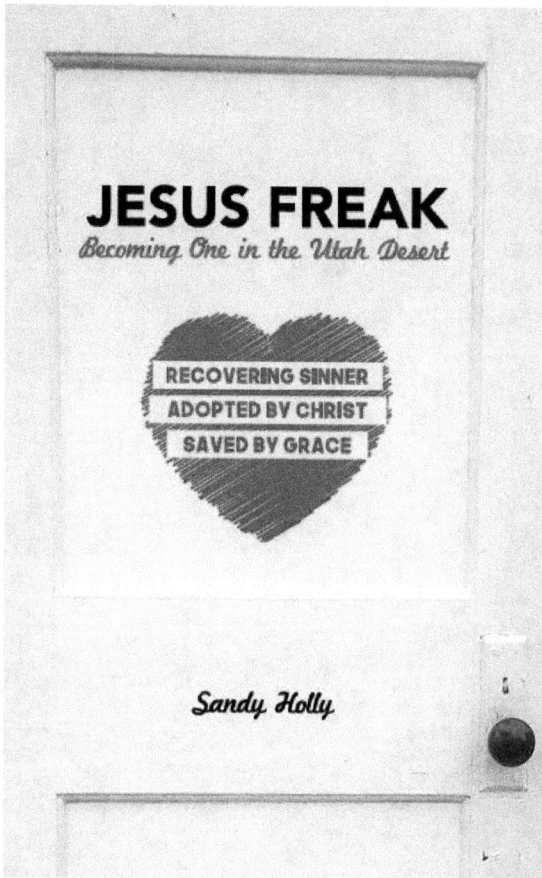

Come on an encouraging adventure in the middle of the Utah desert where God took away my complacent heart, and replaced it with a new compassionate one. This book came about as I began journaling through my Utah experiences of living and loving God in a place where it appeared others didn't. I was living in a paradox among the Mormons. I experienced a culture unbeknownst to me as well as my quest to know and understand the saving love that is the Christ. This is my story of becoming a "Jesus freak."

Find Your JOY

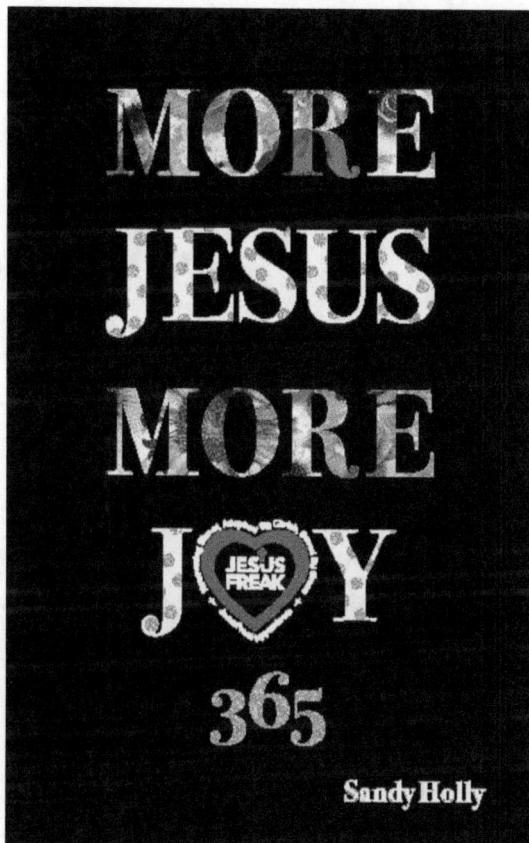

Here's the thing about joy: it's everywhere, and it's ours for the taking. We can choose joy, find it, be in it, and live in it whenever we want. No matter what situation we are facing in life, we can find joy in it. John 10:10 states that Jesus came to give us life and to give it to us more abundantly! That's not a ho-hum kind of existence. It's a freedom and extravagant-joy kind of living! Today, let's throw kindness and joy around like confetti and plug into God who gives us an unlimited amount. Together, let's gather the joys that Jesus so freely gives us and go on the journey for *More Jesus More Joy 365!*

Reading the Bible in a Year has never been easier!

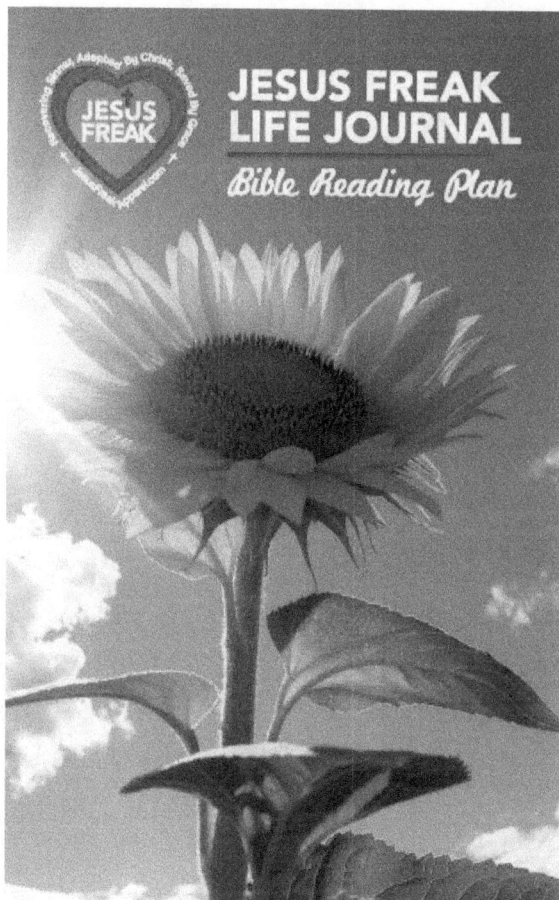

In just twenty minutes a day, you will read the Bible in a year!
The *Jesus Freak Life Journal* Bible-reading plan combines
readings from both the Old and New Testaments daily. Learn
to journal your way through the Bible using the *SOAP* method
of reading and applying Scriptures to your daily life. Available
at JesusFreakApparel.com.

Yahoo! It's Time to Tell Your Story!

In your own Personal Journal available at
JesusFreakApparel.com

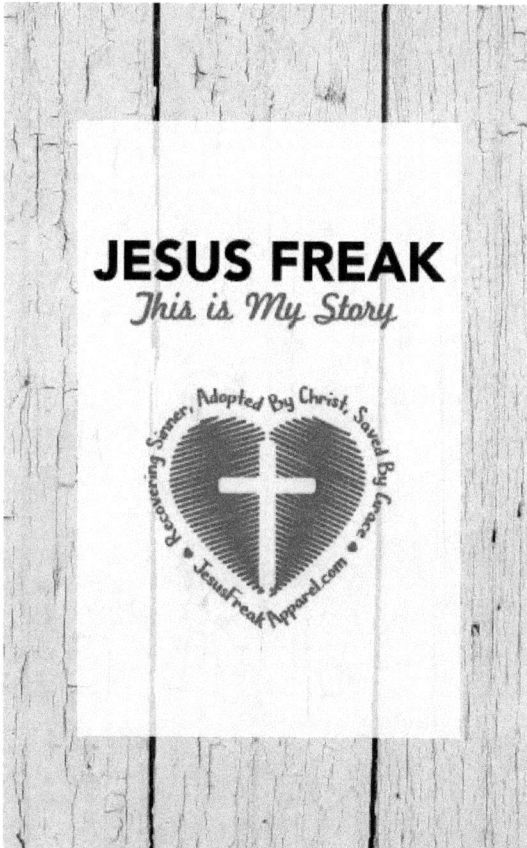

Everyone has a story to tell. May I encourage you to write your story and explore your life? Journaling your personal experience is a way of organizing your thoughts and helps you remember the character of God. You will find the places where God has shown up in the most beautiful ways. It was through journaling that God had the opportunity to grow and shape me. Will you let Him shape you?

www.ingramcontent.com/pod-product-compliance
Lightning Source LLC
LaVergne TN
LVHW051512080426
835509LV00017B/2036